PREPARING TO BE LUCKY

A Public and Private Life Shaped by Humor

Arnold I. Burns

Library of Congress Control Number:		2006909431
ISBN:	Hardcover	978-1-4257-4026-9
	Softcover	978-1-4257-4025-2

This book was printed in the United States of America.

To order additional copies of this book, contact:
Xlibris Corporation
1-888-795-4274
www.Xlibris.com
Orders@Xlibris.com
35955

Contents

The caricature on the cover of the author and his wife, Felice, was done in 1998 by the great Al Hirschfeld.

This book was written for and is dedicated to our three grandchildren, Brendan, Scott and Leah.

INTRODUCTION

Preparing with Humor

Everyone wants to be successful. Yes, we place great value—"a premium"—on success. My dictionary defines success as "the achievement of something desired, planned or attempted" and "the gaining of fame or prosperity." It also tells us that Emily Dickinson wrote "Success is counted sweetest/By those who ne'er succeed." Tomes have been written about how to succeed. A magazine that bore the name *Success* itself failed and filed for bankruptcy. A humorous play was written about how to succeed in business without even trying.

For anyone who wishes to achieve a particular goal whatever it may be or who wishes to gain celebrity status or who wishes to amass wealth or who wishes to excel in a given field whether in business, in academe, in sports, in music or in the other arts we share the advice that Dean Rusk gave to a group of high school students. One of them asked: "Mr. Rusk, you have been President of Chicago University, led the Ford Foundation and served as Secretary of State of the United States. To what do you attribute your enormous success?" Rusk responded with: "That's easy. Every single day of my life I prepared myself to be lucky."

Gary Player, the great golfer, put it this way: "The harder I practice, the luckier I get." Benjamin Franklin said, "Diligence is the mother of good luck." Paderewski, the renowned pianist, once explained that he practiced faithfully every day. "If I miss one day's practice," he said, "I notice it. If I miss two days, the critics notice it. If I miss three days, the audience notices it."

When the Athenian sculptor Phidias was carving the statue of Athena to be placed in the Acropolis and was working on the back of her head, he was careful to bring out with his chisel every strand of hair, as far as possible. Someone watching remarked: "That figure is to stand a hundred feet high, with its back to the marble wall. Who will ever know what details you are putting behind there?" Phidias answered, "I will know." And he continued with his detailed chiseling.

There's a kernel of truth in the classic story of the stranger who walking on 57th Street and Fifth Avenue in New York City asks a lady pedestrian, "How do you get to Carnegie Hall?" (Located nearby on 57th and Seventh.) She responds with "Practice. Practice. Practice!"

I have always tried to give 100 percent effort to every task undertaken. And after the 100 percent is done, to throw an additional 10 percent effort into the project.

Yes, hard work and total commitment and dedication to your desired goal is important. A representative of a learned society called on Jean Louis Agassiz, the noted 19th-century Swiss naturalist, to invite him to address its members. Agassiz refused on the grounds that lectures of this sort took up too much time that should be devoted to research and writing. The man persisted, saying that they were prepared to pay handsomely for the talk. "That's no inducement to me," Agassiz replied. "I can't afford to waste my time making money."

The late Charles Luckman was a good friend of mine. He served as a member of the Board of Directors of Freedoms Foundation at Valley Forge, which I was privileged to chair. Chuck was extraordinarily successful in not one but two careers. When he graduated from college with an architectural degree during the Great Depression of the 1930's, he couldn't get a job in his chosen field. The only employment he could find was as a toothpaste salesman. He wound up as CEO of the giant Lever Brothers. After his career in industry, he turned once more to architecture and became a very successful architect with a hugely lucrative business. Chuck said, "Success is that old ABC—ability, breaks and courage."

Helen F. Boehm, of Boehm porcelain fame, is a good friend. Helen and I served together on the Board of Directors of the National Center for Missing and Exploited Children. By any standard of measurement, Helen has been enormously successful. Her view:

> "Anyone who says success is easy to achieve has his head buried in the sand. There is luck—and then there is WORK! Whoever sees that the sweat of hard work and a dogged refusal to be stopped brings enormous happiness and satisfaction has 20-20 vision."

To make the point that luck alone cannot be relied on for success, there is no better story than the one about the pious man who devoted his life to the study of the Scriptures and performance of all of God's commandments. He sacrificed a secular career and the accumulation of wealth in order to devote himself to a life of piety. When his state adopted a lottery, he saw an opportunity to finally provide for the material well-being of his family without taking time away from prayer, study and the performance of God's commandments. Each day the man fervently prayed to God for the good luck to win the lottery. But each day his prayer went unanswered. Finally, one day in the midst of his most fervent and intensive prayer, the man heard a voice in his mind: "My good fellow, meet me halfway. Buy a ticket!"

This book is not an autobiography. It does, however, contain a number of vignettes of my life's experience. I consider myself to have been extraordinarily lucky in the rearing of a fine family, in my chosen profession, in philanthropic endeavors, and in the political arena. But as you will see, I have to confess that I frequently prepared myself to be lucky. So this book's message is "the key to success is hard work, elbow grease, boning up, guts, commitment, perseverance and dedication."

But there is something more. The chances of success can be improved mightily by maintaining a sense of humor. Take your job, your task, your project seriously—very seriously. But for heaven's sake, *do not take yourself too seriously*. A newly appointed bishop, received by His Holiness, Pope John XXIII, in a private audience, complained that the burden of his new office prevented him from sleeping. "Oh," said the Pope, kindly. "The very same thing happened to me in the first week of my pontificate, but then one day my guardian angel appeared to me in a daydream and whispered, 'Giovanni, don't take yourself so seriously, try laughing at yourself;' and ever since, I've been able to sleep."

This volume contains numerous examples of humor, which, if used properly, can help you lighten up. There are stories, jokes and anecdotes containing Washington, D.C., humor, Ronald Reagan's humor, Department of Justice humor, political humor, college humor, army humor, kids humor, Jewish humor, marital humor, lawyer's humor, desert humor and my own sense of humor.

These stories can be very useful in:

- ✓ breaking the ice with an audience, whether in a public address, business presentation, or a conversation in a social setting;
- ✓ getting an audience on your side from the get-go;
- ✓ relaxing your audience and making them receptive to the information you wish to impart;
- ✓ relaxing you and making you feel at home with your audience;
- ✓ holding their attention by punctuating your remarks with humor, recognizing that most audiences have the span of attention of a flea;
- ✓ slipping your audience your message in a painless way for both of you;
- ✓ entertaining your audience so that a good time is had by all;
- ✓ using an amusing anecdote or joke or story to make or illustrate a point much as I have done so far in this introductory chapter, and as I will continue to do through the rest of this volume; and
- ✓ facilitating your getting along with others.

Theodore Roosevelt, our twenty-sixth President, said: "The most important single ingredient in the formula of success is knowing how to get along with people."

A few years ago I had the occasion to make some remarks at a dinner held in the National Capitol in Washington, D.C., under the auspices of the International Centre for Missing & Exploited Children. The audience was cool. Its members were hungry. They had no interest at all in any speechifying. I started by offering each and every one of them a warm and hearty welcome to the historic Capitol building. I told them that according to Ron Nessen, former White House Press Secretary, no one in Washington, D.C., believes an official spokesperson, but everyone trusts and believes an unidentified source. They laughed. I said that, with their permission, I would address my few words to them not as an official spokesman but as an "unidentified source." I had their attention.

I then delivered my "commercial" message. I ticked off the many accomplishments of the Centre and outlined the important global projects in which it is engaged. I made a pitch for support and additional financial resources.

I then told the story of the newcomer to Washington, D.C., who was riding in a taxi down Constitution Avenue. When the cab passed the archives building, he noticed the phrase etched in stone, "Past is Prologue." He asked the cabbie what that meant. The driver replied, "Oh, that's just bureaucratic talk for 'you ain't seen nothin yet.'" I concluded by reminding them that I was an "unidentified source" and exclaiming that "you ain't seen nothin yet." I sat down amid laughter.

So if you are interested in improving your chances of achieving success by preparing yourself to be lucky—with the help of a treasury of humorous stories, anecdotes, and jokes, dear reader, pray read on.

CHAPTER 1

Humor in the Capital—Amid a Crisis

Washington, D.C., has been described as 67 square miles surrounded by reality. It also has been noted for its Southern efficiency and Northern hospitality.

"Mr. President, I came to Washington as a Reagan man. I am going home a Reagan man. There is nothing I would not do for you. If you asked me to put a broom up my ass and run up and down the halls of the White House to sweep the floors, I would do it. But, the one thing I cannot do is remain in the Department of Justice so long as Ed Meese continues as Attorney General."

That was me speaking to Ronald Reagan, President of the United States—Chief Magistrate of our nation. The place—the small room off the Oval Office in the White House. The date—April 21st, 1988. Duration of the meeting—40 minutes. *Dramatis personae:* President Reagan; Vice President George H. W. Bush (to succeed Reagan as forty-first President of the United States); A. B. Culvahouse, Counsel to the President; Senator Howard Baker, Chief of Staff to the President; William F. Weld, then Assistant Attorney General in charge of the Criminal Division of the Department of Justice (to be elected Governor of Massachusetts as the Republican candidate in 1990); and me. Before the meeting started in earnest, the official White House photographer snapped a picture of the group.

The President had a good laugh—a guffaw—over my remark to him about the broom. In his book, *President Reagan the Role of a Lifetime*, Lou Cannon, the respected Reagan biographer, recounts this "broom" story, which he vetted with a number of participants at the meeting. Cannon's account is accurate, except that he substituted the word "behind" for "ass," I guess to clean it up a bit.

But why were we all assembled there? On January 6th, 1986, I was sworn in as Associate Attorney General of the United States (the third ranking member of the Justice Department), following my nomination by the President and confirmation by the United States Senate. Then I was promoted. On July 24th, 1986, I was sworn in as Deputy Attorney General of the United States (the number two person in the Justice Department and its Chief Operating Officer), again, after nomination by the President and confirmation by the United States Senate. But on March 29th, 1988, I resigned from the Department of Justice. On April 22nd, 1988, I left my post. Bill Weld, resigned with me on March 29th. Bill left his post on the day we resigned. I remained at the Department for another month at the specific request of the Attorney General who asked me to stay on and run the Department in his absence, as he had a long-planned governmental business trip abroad.

We were assembled at the White House at the request of the President, to explain to him why we had resigned. I led off by explaining to the group that I personally liked Ed Meese, the Attorney General. We had a fine personal relationship. His wife Ursula and I had become friends while serving together on the Board of Directors at the Freedoms Foundation at Valley Forge which I was privileged to chair. Ed and Ursula had been weekend guests at our summer home in Westhampton Beach on Long Island on two separate occasions. We had a few of our neighbors in for drinks and Ed, on his own motion, acted as bartender. He was a regular guy. Contrary to opinions held by some detractors, he was bright and had a fine legal mind. He had a deep understanding of legal and policy issues. He was a hands-on leader. Key personnel at Justice met every morning at 8 a.m. Ed was accessible to his people. The Department was well run under his leadership. That was the upside.

The downside. He had become a political lightning rod, and the Department increasingly appeared to be highly politicized. Meese had been Ronald Reagan's Chief of Staff for 6 of the eight years of Reagan's governorship of California. He was one of Reagan's top political aides in the White House. When he moved from 1600 Pennsylvania Avenue to Justice at 10th and Constitution Avenue, in my view, Ed failed to fully appreciate the need to shed the garb of the political gladiator for the robe of the impartial administrator of justice.

In March of 1987, during a weekend I was spending with Ed Meese at a Justice Department Conference in Annapolis, Maryland, I received a telephone call from Bill Weld in which he shared with me information he had received from Rudy Giuliani, then the United States Attorney in the Southern District of New York. I learned that there were serious allegations against the Attorney General growing out of the investigation of the Wedtech Corporation. E. Robert Wallach, a close personal friend of Ed Meese, was implicated as was the Attorney General himself.

Members of Congress asked the Justice Department to conduct a preliminary investigation of Mr. Meese in accordance with the provisions of the Ethics in Government Act. As the investigation got underway, I learned of a half dozen separate allegations of serious wrongdoing by the Attorney General. The public integrity section of the Department of Justice and Assistant Attorney General Bill Weld advised me, as Acting Attorney General, that there was evidence that the Attorney General may have violated the criminal laws of the United States and *that further investigation was required*. Under the Ethics in Government Act, the Attorney General (in this case, the Acting Attorney General) *is required* to apply for the appointment of an independent counsel unless within 90 days after the trigger of the preliminary investigation, he makes a determination that there are no reasonable grounds to believe that further investigation or prosecution is warranted. I could make no such determination in view of the unequivocal advice I had received that *further investigation was required*.

Accordingly, on May 11th, 1987, as Acting Attorney General, I asked James C. McKay, the court appointed Independent Counsel, to undertake an independent investigation of Mr. Meese. I took this step only after consulting with others in the Department including Charles Cooper, Assistant Attorney General in charge of the Office of Legal Counsel, for whom I had the greatest respect and in whose judgment I had great confidence.

As I later had the occasion to state publicly: "I can tell you that it was not a happy moment for me. It was not a pleasant decision. I did not like it one bit."

During the year following the March 1987 surfacing of the allegations against the Attorney General, the morale, performance and public perception of the Department deteriorated greatly. As Deputy Attorney General, I had contact with all facets of the Department of Justice. I had supervision over the 94 United States Attorneys, the FBI, DEA, Bureau of Prisons, INS, the United States Marshals, the Criminal Division and all of the civil divisions of the Department, and so many other components of the Department. I met regularly with the leadership of the Department and with career attorneys and personnel across the board. In short, I was in a unique position to measure morale and performance of the Department.

I could see the performance of the Department of Justice was being impeded. The Department's great record was being eroded by a deep malaise setting in because of Mr. Meese's problems. Graffiti containing slurs like "crook" and "pig" appeared in the halls of the Department. A federal prosecutor in New York, in a federal courthouse, in a federal prosecution, on two occasions, called the Attorney General of the United States a "sleaze."

It was with this background one year later that I explained to the President and Vice President that my decision to resign was not based on any hard feelings or personal animus toward the Attorney General. I believed that with serious unresolved allegations of criminal conduct swirling about him, Mr. Meese could not continue to act as Attorney General. I believed that at the very least, he should have stepped aside and taken administrative leave until the Independent Counsel completed his investigation and delivered his report.

I also knew that Bill Weld, who as United States Attorney in Boston, Massachusetts, had compiled an enviable record of obtaining over 108 convictions out of the 111 public corruption prosecutions he authorized, had concluded that, if the decision were his, he would seek Mr. Meese's indictment.

During my presentation, the President and Vice President were very attentive. The President was ashen. The Vice President was florid and visibly upset. I spoke for about 15 minutes. I was followed by Bill Weld, who spoke for over 20 minutes. Bill delivered a brilliant painstaking analysis of the facts and the law with particular emphasis on the gratuity statute. Bill was crystal clear in stating that if the decision were his, he would seek the Attorney General's indictment!

Here is Lou Cannon's take on our White House meeting:

> Their forty-minute meeting with the President and Vice President was one of the most revealing in the Reagan presidency. Burns was both blunt and theatrical . . . Burns had warned Meese a year earlier that his relationship with Wallach gave the impression of a conflict of interest. Meese had ignored him, and the conflicts had grown worse. Burns said he liked Meese but thought that he had been "hornswoggled and bamboozled" by Wallach (who would later be convicted for his role in the Wedtech scandal.) Burns added solemnly that "the temple of justice" had been besmirched by Meese's conduct . . . Bush twice interrupted to ask questions of Burns. When he inquired about morale at the Justice Department, Burns told him it was at its nadir, the lowest "probably since the founding of the republic."
>
> By the time Weld spoke, in a less animated presentation, Reagan was fading. Two of the participants in the meeting told me that the president nodded off while Weld was speaking to him. And what Weld had to say was important. He told Reagan that if it were left to him he would seek an indictment of Meese, probably the first time in history that a political appointee who headed the Justice Department's Criminal Division told a President that his Attorney General should be prosecuted. Reagan did not respond.

As we were leaving the meeting, Bill Weld turned to me and said something like, "Arnie, you are the greatest. You had the President on the edge of his chair the whole time you spoke. When I made my presentation he fell asleep."

I was convinced then, and I remain convinced today, that the difference in the President's listening attentively to me and nodding off during Bill's presentation was attributable to the way I grabbed his attention at the outset with the reference to the broom. Intuitively, I knew Reagan, a man's man, would react favorably. I never would have used that intro with say, President George H. W. Bush. I surely would have used it with President Lyndon Johnson. And, I would not have used it in addressing President Harry Truman notwithstanding that he was known all his life for his plain speaking. Once when he made a speech at the Washington Garden Club, he kept referring to the "good manure" that needed to be used on the flowers. Some society women complained to his wife, Bess. "Couldn't you get the President to say 'fertilizer'?" they asked. Mrs. Truman replied, "Heavens no. It took me twenty-five years to get him to say 'manure.'"

I think it important to note that our resignations were not the result of spur of the moment decisions and were not sprung as a surprise to the White House. Prior to the announcement of our resignations, Bill Weld and I met on three occasions with A. B. Culvahouse, White House Counsel, and on two occasions with Senator Howard Baker the President's Chief of Staff. We shared with them our thought processes.

Following our resignations in March 1988, I was besieged by calls from newspapers, magazines, radio stations and television programs. No surprise. They wanted the inside story. Prior to my testimony before the Senate Judiciary Committee on July 26th, 1988, I kept my own counsel about my reasons for leaving the Department of Justice. I refused all media interviews. I told everyone who asked, including the Senate Judiciary Committee, that I would maintain "radio silence" until such time as Independent Counsel McKay published the report of his investigation. I did this because I did not want to run the risk of prejudicing Mr. Meese insofar as Mr. McKay's investigation was concerned.

Mr. McKay issued his report on July 15th, 1988. On July 26th, 1988, Bill Weld and I appeared before the Judiciary Committee of the United States Senate. We were advised by the Committee that we needn't testify under oath. But each of us insisted on being sworn with our testimony subject to the penalties for perjury.

The practice, when testifying before Congress, is to submit a written statement of what you are going to say. That statement is part of the record. When you appear in person, you can enlarge upon, abridge or otherwise modify your written statement. In my written submission, as well as in my actual presentation before the Committee, I explained why I left the Department of Justice when I did. In essence, I repeated and expanded upon what I had told the President and Vice President at our meeting in April. When I testified in person, quite spontaneously and entirely extemporaneously, I adlibbed, saying:

> So you get the flavor of what life was like in the Department of Justice, this gives you some idea. It was a world of Alice in Wonderland, a world of illusion and allusion, a world in which up was down and down was

up, in was out and out was in, happy was sad and sad was happy, rain was sunshine, sunshine was rain, hot was cold and cold was hot.

In my written statement I did *not* include any reference to Alice in Wonderland. These two sentences, out of testimony lasting three hours, captured the imagination of America. Cartoons appeared all over the country, some depicting Mr. Meese and other members of the Washington scene as characters in *Alice's Adventures in Wonderland*." I purchased four original cartoons which today hang in the den of my son Doug's home on Long Island's north shore.

Newspapers around the country carried front page stories, with photographs of Bill and me at the hearing, about our resignations.

The *Washington Post*, (Wednesday, July 27th, 1988) under the caption, "Justice Department was World of Alice in Wonderland," reported:

> The Justice Department's former second-ranking official yesterday described the department under Attorney General Edwin Meese III as a "world of Alice in Wonderland" in which Meese perceived no problem with his conduct, while the former criminal division chief said Meese would have been indicted if he had been an "ordinary public official." In an extraordinary, three-hour appearance before the Senate Judiciary Committee, former Deputy Attorney General Arnold I. Burns and former Assistant Attorney General William F. Weld detailed for the first time publicly the reasons for their abrupt resignations.

The *New York Times* in its reporting included a lengthy excerpt from my testimony. Ron Ostrow, in his front page story in the *Los Angeles Times*, reported the following under the headline, "Meese in Justice Department Seen as an 'Alice in Wonderland'":

> The Justice Department's former top prosecutor laid out publicly for the first time Tuesday the criminal case he believed should have been brought against Atty. Gen. Edwin Meese III for accepting gratuities from E. Robert Wallach allegedly in return for official actions he took that benefited his longtime friend . . . Former Deputy Atty. General Arnold I. Burns . . . told the Senate panel that Meese lives at the Justice Department in "an Alice in Wonderland world . . . of illusion." "If Mr. Meese were given a shot of sodium pentothal," Burns said, referring to the chemical commonly known as truth serum, he would "cling to the thought that he committed no crime . . . no wrong . . . no act of impropriety . . . no ethical violation . . . no error of good taste or bad taste, that he comported himself properly [and] if he had to do over again, he would comport himself in the same way."

I do not know—I will never know—what prompted the reference to Alice in Wonderland. I guess it just happened.

Bill testified in unambiguous terms:

> My professional opinion was . . . the facts . . . also ran afoul of the Federal gratuity law, 18 U.S.C. 201, which is a two-year felony provision applicable to anybody who "directly or indirectly gives, offers or promises anything of value to any public official for or because of any official act performed or to be performed by such public official," or anyone who "being a public official directly or indirectly receives, accepts, or agrees to receive or accept anything of value personally because of any official act performed or to be performed by such official." . . . I did conclude that if these facts had been presented to me as a U.S. attorney in Boston . . . I would have approved the case for prosecution.

As already mentioned, on July 15th, 1988, James C. McKay as the Independent Counsel issued an 814 page report. He concluded that Mr. Meese probably violated four provisions of the criminal laws of the United States. Notwithstanding probable cause to seek an indictment, he declined to do so as a matter of prosecutorial discretion.

In January 1989, the Office of Professional Responsibility of the Justice Department, charged with the task of investigating allegations of wrongdoing by Department employees, issued a 61 page report. On January 17th, 1985, the *Washington Post*, under the headline, "Mr. Meese's Disgrace," said:

> The difference between escaping indictment and vindication has long eluded Edwin Meese. He claimed vindication when one special prosecutor failed to indict him, thus clearing the way for his confirmation as Attorney General. He claimed vindication again last summer when another special prosecutor declined to file criminal charges. Now the Justice Department's own ethical watchdog, the respected Office of Professional Responsibility, reasserts the critical distinction. Concluding its 61-page review of an independent counsel's report, that office says:
>
>> "We trust that this analysis will lay to rest the claims by Mr. Meese that the appropriate standard for official behavior is whether an independent counsel seeks an official's indictment. We found that the independent counsel's report far from vindicates Mr. Meese; rather, it details conduct which should not be tolerated of any government employee, especially not the Attorney General of the

> United States. Were he still serving as Attorney General, we would recommend . . . that the President take disciplinary action."

Is there a lesson in all this? Is there a point in recounting this story. I think so.

The point is that public servants—those entrusted with public business—must have a high sensitivity not only to impropriety but to the appearance of impropriety as well. When shortcuts are taken—when corners are cut—when questionable conduct becomes subject to public scrutiny, inevitably there is an erosion of the public confidence in our system of government. And when this occurs, we must be ready, willing and able to take action to remedy the situation.

CHAPTER 2

Alice in Wonderland at Justice

The jury foreman was asked by the bailiff if he should send in twelve dinners as usual. "No," said the foreman, "Make it eleven dinners and a bale of hay."

A brand new customs inspector, with his supervisor at his side was clearing incoming passengers at JFK. At his request, a homecoming passenger opened his attaché case to reveal a box of 50 beautiful and expensive Cuban cigars. Flustered, the youngster turned to his senior for guidance:

"These are illegal—against the law. They are contraband. They must be confiscated. They must be burned—S—L—O—W—L—Y—one by one."

A man walked into a public library and asked whether they had a copy of the French constitution. The librarian responded by saying no, we do not keep periodicals here.

A cartoon in the New Yorker *magazine years ago depicted a man walking down the stairs of the United States Courthouse in New York City with photographers all around him snapping pictures. The man is hiding behind his fedora which is covering his face. A man walking beside him says, "For God's sake, Joe, remember you're a public official now."*

The decision to resign as the number two person at the Justice Department was not by any means one made on the spur of the moment. In November of 1987, I took an official trip to the Philippines (including the island fortress of Corregidor), Cambodia, Singapore, Brunei and Malaysia. During the trip I had some reflective time. I realized that I would have to leave Justice lest my continued presence be construed as condoning Mr. Meese's conduct. En route we stopped on the island of Guam. In our party was the late Alan Nelson, then Commissioner of Immigration and Naturalization, who addressed a group and told the following story which I have used many times since:

> A young man entered a monastic order taking vows of poverty and silence. Under the prescribed rules he was entitled to speak two words every seven years. For the first seven years, he performed hard labor daily and spent his spare time in silent devotions, meditations and prayer. After seven years, he went to the Abbott and said, "Bed hard."
>
> He then toiled under the same harsh regimen for another seven years. On the fourteenth anniversary of his ordination he went to the Abbott and said, "Food lousy."
>
> Back he went into his regimen of silence hard work, meditation, devotion and prayer for another seven years, at which point he went to the Abbott and said, "I quit." To which the Abbott responded, "I'm not surprised. All you have done since you have arrived is bitch and moan, bitch and moan."

Early in 1988, the Justice Department held its annual conference of United States Attorneys at the Grant Hotel in San Diego, California. There were 94 United States Attorneys, and the get-together was very well attended. I was the keynote speaker. Typically, I would have talked about serious and substantive issues with which we were grappling in the Department of Justice, such as tort reform, the battle against drugs (prevention, interdiction, indictment, prosecution, incarceration, rehabilitation), pornography and the sexual exploitation of children, to name a few. On this occasion I did not do so. My talk was wholly without substance. Instead of a thoughtful, reasoned, motivational speech, I delivered a very humorous after dinner speech peppered with funny stories, anecdotes and jokes. My purpose was to signal the fact that my mind was no longer on day-to-day Justice Department business but on the overarching issues presented by the fact that the chief lawyer of our nation—the Attorney General—was under allegations of serious misconduct. I do not think my message was received or understood. It was a little too subtle, I am afraid.

I cannot remember all of the stories I told, but I do recall mentioning that two of San Diego's best known attractions are the world famous San Diego Zoo and Del Mar Racetrack. And, I said that one of our United States Attorneys had come to the conference early and brought his family with him to San Diego. During free time before the conference began, our colleague's wife insisted that her husband take their six-year old daughter to the zoo. He grudgingly agreed. That evening his wife asked her daughter how she liked the zoo. "Oh, Mommy," replied the little tot, "the zoo was wonderful! The best was when daddy started jumping up and down after one of the animals paid $22.80!"

At prior conferences and meetings I would try to inspire:

> Let me share with you a parable I heard Justice Robert Jackson tell in 1950. "Once upon a time, three stonemasons were asked, one after the other, what they were doing. The first, without looking up, answered, 'earning my living.' The second replied, 'I am shaping this stone to pattern.' The third lifted his eyes and said, 'I am building a cathedral.' So it is with the men of the law who labor in its vineyards. So it is with U.S. Attorneys in leadership positions. We want inspired men and women who have a conception of their efforts higher than plying a trade, or shaping cases to a winning pattern. We want men and women who will throw their managerial, litigation, professional, people and leadership skills into the breach with the knowledge that they are helping the President *build a cathedral.*"

To instruct:

> A period of adjustment is required, which brings to mind the story of a group such as your own, not former United States attorneys, but a convention of former pirates, people who made their living plundering on the high seas. At their reunion, one pirate turned to another and said, "Blackbeard, what happened to you? You used to be such a robust man, and I see that you've got a wooden leg." "Well," the other man responded, "I was in a ferocious battle and a cannonball blew through

the side of my frigate and shattered my leg, but I am used to it now and doing well." His friend said, "But Blackbeard, you used to have hands like ham hocks, and now I see you have a steel hook. What happened?" Blackbeard said, "Well, in another fierce battle I was dueling and just before I killed my adversary, he sliced my hand off, but I am getting on very well." His friend said, "But you had such beautiful piercing blue eyes, and I see that you now have a patch on one of your eyes. What happened?" Blackbeard responded by saying, "One night I was on watch in the crow's next, and I was looking up and an albatross flew by and dropped something right in my eye, and I lost my eye." His friend said, "My lord, that can't possibly account for losing your eye." Blackbeard responded by saying, "It can when you realize that it happened the first day I had my new hook." So you can see, a period of adjustment is necessary."

To caution:

The small son of a mountaineer was accosted by a revenuer.

"Where's your pappy?" asked the officer.
"Pappy's up at the still."
"Where's your mother?"
"She's up at the still, too."
"I'll give you a dollar," said the officer, "if you'll take me up there."
"All right," said the boy, "give me the dollar."
"I'll give it to you when we get back," said the officer.
"No, sir, mister, give it to me now," insisted the boy.
"You ain't a comin' back."

While at the San Diego conference, my wife Felice chatted with Bill Weld. She told him that I was pretty close to tendering my resignation. She asked him what his thinking was. He responded by saying, "Arnie is a few weeks ahead of me in his thinking, but I am in the fast lane catching up quickly."

How did I happen to become Deputy Attorney General of the United States? I did not seek the job. I did not aspire to the job. I did not maneuver to get the job. I never thought about the job. My getting the job was a complete fluke.

I was asked to deliver the keynote address at the annual conference of Boys & Girls Clubs of America held in San Juan, Puerto Rico, in the spring of 1985. I did so. I have no recollection whatever of what I said. Apparently, whatever I said, I said very well. I had carefully prepared my remarks. In fact, I prepared myself to be lucky, following Dean Rusk's example.

One of the people in the audience, Jeremiah Milbank, who was President of Boys & Girls Clubs of America and who had been a big wig fundraiser for the Republican Party, wrote a personal letter to the Attorney General recommending that I be appointed Solicitor General of the United States, the fourth ranking person in the Department of Justice. Milbank, not a lawyer, received an acknowledgment, thanking him for *his* interest in joining the Department of Justice, advising him that there were no job openings, but that his letter would be kept on file and assuring him he would be contacted if an opening developed. Milbank found this amusing in the extreme and showed the letter to E. Pendleton James, a friend of Milbank's and a close friend of Ed and Ursula Meese's. Pen was in the headhunting business and quite successful at it. In fact, when Ronald Reagan was first elected President, Pen had the job in the administration of staffing it. Pen thought the Milbank letter amusing and took it to Washington and shared it with Ed Meese. As I understand it, he asked Ed, in effect, what kind of a horse's ass was he and what kind of a Mickey Mouse operation was he running? Ed responded by saying he knew Arnie Burns and that he would like to talk to him about the possibility of Burns' joining the Department of Justice.

I had met Ed at functions held under the auspices of the Republican Senatorial Trust of which I was a member. As its name suggests, it funded Republican candidates for the United States Senate; I also knew Ed through my work as Chairman of the Freedoms Foundation at Valley Forge; I met with him as an active member of the Board of Boys & Girls Clubs of America; and I ran into him at various Republican gatherings. I was summoned to Washington, and I was interviewed by a half dozen people in the Department. I apparently passed muster. The Attorney General offered me the job of Associate Attorney General, the third ranking post in the Department. He told me in no uncertain terms that there was *no chance* of promotion because the incumbent Deputy Attorney General, Lowell Jenson, was not going anywhere. I accepted the job.

Shortly after assuming my duties at the Department and while I was still breaking in, I received a phone call from James Baker, then the Secretary of the Treasury. He said he had a legal problem. I told him I made house calls and would be right over. He informed me that he had two planes in Hawaii loaded with Ferdinand Marcos and his wife Imelda, an entourage and loads of securities, gold, currency and other things of value. The threshold problem: The Marcoses claim the stuff is theirs; the Philippine government says it all belongs to the Philippines. What do we do? Second issue: what do we do with the Marcoses. How do we keep them under surveillance and prevent them from stirring up trouble? Third issue: There are a number of lawsuits pending against the Marcoses around the country. How do we handle them?

I counseled Treasury. The Attorney General tasked me with the job of looking after all Marcos issues. I did so. Apparently, I was perceived to have done a good job. The Attorney General told me Lowell Jenson was being appointed to the federal bench in San Francisco and he wanted me to become Deputy Attorney General. Again, I had prepared myself to be lucky.

When I testified before the Judiciary Committee, this is what I had to say about my experience at the Department of Justice:

> I came to Washington, D. C., to the Department of Justice, from the active practice of law. I have now practiced law for thirty-five years. I was fortunate, I was lucky, to have founded and headed a firm which today numbers over one hundred lawyers.
>
> When the opportunity came, and came unexpectedly, for me to serve my country, I did not hesitate for a moment. Many of my friends and colleagues told me I was crazy, nuts, to sever my relationship with a lucrative law practice to come serve my government. I disagreed. They were wrong; I was right.
>
> The opportunity to serve this great Nation, to serve President Reagan and his administration, and to make a contribution, however small, to the improvement of the administration of justice, was unique.
>
> I thought I had won the Irish Sweepstakes when I was selected for the job.
>
> As I look back, and as you can imagine, I have now had ample time for reflection, I can say without reservation that my tenure at the Department of Justice was the highlight of my professional life.
>
> I think being Deputy Attorney General of the United States, as Senator Leahy suggested, has got to be one of the greatest jobs in the world for any lawyer. The opportunity to act as chief operating officer, and to run on a day-to-day basis the Justice Department, the largest law firm in the history of the world, and to have hands-on responsibility for management of roughly 65,000 people, and to deal with issues that cover the whole spectrum of law, of policy, of management, was an opportunity of a lifetime.
>
> And to do so with a cadre of professional men and women who work in the Department of Justice, people who are responsible for the great record that Senator Hatch referred to in his statement, the opportunity to work with these people, some of the finest, and most

> dedicated, and most competent lawyers, and people, I have ever met, was a great privilege.
>
> I loved the job. I loved working with the people. I loved working the problems. I loved working the issues. You can now imagine that my decision to leave the Department of Justice was made with a heavy heart.
>
> Mr. Chairman, the day I left was one of the saddest days of my life.

No doubt. The legal talent in the Department was tops. A-One. First rate. We dealt with difficult and important issues. I had to decide whether to challenge or support the constitutionality of the Ethics in Government Act (the independent counsel statute) and separately, the Sentencing Commission established by the Congress and the Commission's Sentencing Guidelines. I had to pass on the settlement of the tort claims on behalf of the families of the astronauts killed in the Challenger tragedy. I had to approve the settlement of all cases against the Government which involved an outlay of more than $300,000. I had to deal with the Department's budget. There were all kinds of personnel issues. Supervision of all the agencies of the Department, the United States Attorneys and all the Criminal and Civil Divisions, among so many other responsibilities fell within my jurisdiction. I, too, had a bully pulpit and gave public speeches from Maine to Florida and New York to California.

I could not have discharged my responsibilities without the active, competent assistance of a whole cadre of lawyers. My principal deputy during my entire time at the Department was Randy Levine, who was an associate in the labor department of my law firm in New York. I selected Randy from a group of over one hundred lawyers. Why did I do so? Years ago I attended an annual national conference of Boys Clubs of America (now Boys & Girls Clubs of America) in Dallas, Texas. The keynote speaker was Tom Landry, coach of the then champion Dallas Cowboys. I was initially skeptical about learning anything of real value from a football coach. To my astonishment, Landry delivered one of the best and most memorable talks I have ever heard. He told us what qualities he looked for in a member of the Cowboys. He said size, strength, speed, agility and athleticism were important, to be sure. But he went on to say that the single most important trait was character. He wanted men on whom teammates could rely, especially when the going got tough. I never forgot that.

At my law firm, I did not have all that much daily contact with Randy. But in a number of encounters with him it was obvious that he was a man of character. He demonstrated loyalty, integrity and courage of his convictions. No doubt he was my man.

Randy served with great distinction in the Department. He was my right hand. He resigned his high government position the day I did. He joined me and became a partner in the Proskauer firm, one of the great law firms of our nation (now named Proskauer Rose, LLP). He later went on in succession to become Labor Commissioner of the City of New York; Chief Labor Negotiator for Major League Baseball; Deputy Mayor of the City of New York and today, President of the New York Yankees as well as a partner in another prestigious international law firm.

If Randy was my right hand, B. Boykin Rose of South Carolina was my left hand. Boykin had had a rich experience in law enforcement before coming to Justice. He, too, resigned. Post Justice, Boykin joined Randy and me as a partner at Proskauer. From there he returned home to South Carolina and served with great distinction—no surprise—as Director of Public Safety in South Carolina, the head of all of South Carolina law enforcement.

Lee Liberman, a brilliant superstar, also served as one of my deputies. Lee was a founder of the Federalist Society when she was in law school. Lee had clerked for Antonin Scalia when he sat on the Court of Appeals for the District of Columbia. One day I heard that Judge Scalia, now Mr. Justice Scalia, because of his elevation to the bench of the Supreme Court of the United States, had offered Lee the opportunity to be his Supreme Court clerk. I also heard that she had turned Scalia down. I called her in and asked about the situation. She explained that she had turned down the job because of her loyalty to me and because of a sense of obligation to finish her tour in the Department. I released her from any sense of obligation to me or the Department and encouraged her to take the clerkship in the interest of advancing her own career. She left and went to the Supreme Court to assist Scalia. Lee has since gone on to great achievement and serves in a very important post in the George W. Bush administration.

Another of my able deputies was Paul Cassell, who today is a United States District Court Judge in Utah.

My three secretaries, Ann Wyatt, Evelyn Long and Betsy Meadows, were indispensable in our running of the Department.

It is impossible to name all of the key people who made the Department work. Suffice it to say, borrowing a phrase, they, with only a few exceptions, were the best and the brightest.

To emphasize the point, I need only mention that colleagues who served with me in the Department of Justice included John Roberts, now Chief Justice of the Supreme Court of the United States; Samuel Alito, now Associate Justice of the Supreme Court, William Weld who Served as Governor of Massachusetts; Lincoln Almond who served as Governor of Rhode Island; Frank Keating who served as Governor of Oklahoma; Jeff Sessions, who is today a United States Senator representing Alabama; Rudy Giuliani who served as Mayor of New York City; John Bolton who is today the United States Permanent Representative to the

United Nations; and so many others, too numerous to mention, who went on, post Justice, to very distinguished careers in both the private and public sectors.

Early in 1987, William Sessions was sworn in as Director of the FBI to succeed William Webster. During the ceremony at the FBI Building I was seated next to Senator Orrin Hatch (R. Utah). During a brief conversation, Senator Hatch said to me, "Arnie, you are going to be the next appointee to the Supreme Court of the United States." I don't know whether he told that to all the boys but I must say he got my attention. And sometime during the year, before there was any real controversy boiling over about Ed Meese, Pen James told me that the game plan was for Ed Meese to resign in due course and for me to succeed him as Attorney General. Pretty heady stuff. I, of course, knew that all this would go down the drain with my resignation from the Department.

CHAPTER 3

Politics Saved and Served by Humor

When John F. Kennedy, our thirty-fifth President, entertained a group of Nobel Prize-winners at the White House in 1962, he welcomed them as the most distinguished gathering of intellects and talents ever to have dined at the Executive Mansion—"with the possible exception of when Thomas Jefferson dined here alone."

On the Senate floor, where things were obviously getting out of hand, the late Senator Everett Dirksen of Illinois quipped, "A hundred million here, a hundred million there and pretty soon you're talking about real money."

One of the first things I did after being asked to become Associate Attorney General of the United States was to go to see Rudy Giuliani who at the time was the United States Attorney in the Southern District of New York. After all, Rudy had served in Washington as Associate Attorney General. I wanted to pick up a few pointers. I had some important questions for him. Where should I live? Where do I park my car? Where do I take my laundry? Where do I buy my groceries? Key stuff like that.

During my time at the Department of Justice, Rudy and I worked together on any number of important cases. When I became Deputy Attorney General, all 94 United States Attorneys reported to me. We were together on the Wedtech case, the Teamsters Civil Rico case, the P.L.O. expulsion case and others. I developed a healthy respect for him as a lawyer and as a leader. I had no idea that my admiration for him was fully reciprocated. That is, until he asked my advice when he was first thinking about running for Mayor of the City of New York. A number of friends, knowing that Rudy had serious political ambitions, counseled him against running for Mayor. They told him it was a political dead end. My advice was different. I told him that Ed Koch was living proof that the mayoralty was not a dead end. Koch, I told Rudy, was a shoo-in for Governor. I thought he had a lock on the gubernatorial campaign until he stuck his big foot in his mouth during a *Penthouse Magazine* interview in which he, in effect, said upstate people were yokels and did not have the challenging lives that New York City folks led. Rudy took my advice, which he has recalled publicly a number of times since. He asked me to lead his campaign as Chairman. In his recent book, *Leadership*, Rudy writes:

> On a warm night in late June, we met at the Sutton Place apartment of Arnie Burns who at that point was campaign chairman . . . So I made Peter [Powers] campaign manager. Arnie Burns became chairman with increased responsibility, since we needed an older, wiser head around, and Arnie was also a phenomenal fund raiser . . .

When I introduced Rudy to audiences during the campaign, I would frequently say, "What difference does it make who is elected Mayor? We all know the city is wholly unmanageable anyway." I would go on to say, "If we believed that, none of us would be here tonight. The fact is we know good, responsible, effective and efficient government can be brought to our City and Rudy's the man who can do it."

As they say, "the rest is history." Rudy lost his first bid for election in a mighty close race against David Dinkins. The next time out, he beat Dinkins and became mayor. He was reelected.

I have to admit that I take great pride and pleasure in having played a small role in giving Rudy Giuliani to the people of New York City. At Rudy's request, I served on the Commission to Combat Police Corruption and Chaired the New York City Commission for Youth Empowerment Services (summer job employment for youth). For 5 years I served as a member of the Board and Executive Committee of the Economic Development Corporation of the City of New York. All, of course, on a *pro bono* basis.

Iran Contra. Judge Lawrence Walsh was appointed independent counsel to investigate. During the course of the investigation, I was interviewed. The independent counsel wanted to know *what* I knew about the sale of arms to Iran (arms for hostages) and the subsequent diversion of proceeds of the sale to the anti-communists in Nicaragua. He also wanted to know *when* I knew about this. I laughed. I responded by saying that I had read a lot of "who done it" books, I had seen a lot of mystery television programs, and I was a devotee of crime movies. I said that in my view, I had the perfect alibi. I explained that when I learned about it, I was in the presence of all nine Justices of the Supreme Court, the Solicitor General of the United States, the President of the United States, the Vice President and the Attorney General. The place was the White House. All of the persons mentioned were invited luncheon guests of the President. Before lunch we were standing around chatting cocktail talk. I remember talking with the late Justice Byron White who, incidentally, had served as Deputy Attorney General. Justice White explained how isolated and insular was the life of a Supreme Court Justice. He said he had standing instructions to his staff that if anyone telephoned, no matter who, to put the call through because he rarely had the opportunity to talk with folks.

Lunch was delayed. We had some more wine. Lunch was further delayed. The President explained that the Attorney General was detained and would be late. The President summoned us into the dining room. We sat down. I was seated between Justice Scalia on my right and the late Justice Thurgood Marshall on my left. After about 10 minutes elapsed and while we were on our salads, the Attorney General appeared. He explained that he had been holding a press conference at which he shared with the public the unhappy news about the secret diversion of monies to the contras. Justice Scalia erupted with a suitable expletive. We were all stunned.

Yes, mine was an airtight alibi.

One Sunday morning in late Spring, I was happily toiling in my garden and puttering about our home in Westhampton Beach on Long Island when I received a telephone call from the Attorney General. He told me he was scheduled to address a meeting of the American College of Trial Lawyers in California the next day. Something important had just developed which required his presence in Washington. He asked me if I'd be willing to jump on a plane and replace him at the program. I agreed.

When I opened my talk before the aggregation of trial lawyers, I mentioned right off the bat that I was a last-minute pinch hitter. I said that I was tempted to stand up and merely read word for word the well-crafted speech prepared for and by the Attorney General. I confessed that I thought better of it and decided not to do that because I remembered the case of the candidate who was covering a lot of territory in a hurry, as the campaign was nearing its end. His speechwriter was hard pressed to keep up with him. In one town, the writer was still typing the speech when the candidate was introduced. He grabbed the speech out of the typewriter without looking at it, and rushed to the platform.

"Fellow citizens," he said, as he read the speech, "I cannot tell you how happy it makes me to be once more in this, my favorite town in America's heartland, so filled with American tradition and the people who make that tradition, and I slip in some soft soap about how pretty this lousy, flea bitten dump is . . ."

They thought it was funny. I got a good laugh. I broke the ice. I went on to share my own thoughts on topics in which they were interested with emphasis on the need for certain reforms in our tort jurisprudence. My talk was punctuated with other humorous stories but I can't now remember which they were.

During my tenure in Washington, Colin Powell, then a Lieutenant General, was National Security Advisor to the President and presided over meetings of the National Security Council. At one such meeting the issue was whether we should shut down the offices of the Palestine Liberation Office (PLO) in New York and in Washington. Abe Sofaer, then Legal Advisor (top lawyer) of the State Department, was to present the case for permitting the PLOto remain in business here in the United States. I was going to argue the Justice Department position that we shut the PLO down promptly and permanently. Abe had been a Professor of Law at Columbia University and he served with great distinction as a United States District Court Judge in the Southern District of New York. Abe is brilliant. Abe is a good friend. When I argued the Japan Whaling Case before the Supreme Court of the United States on behalf of the Administration, Abe helped prepare me for the argument.

Abe opened the debate. He spoke at great length. He made a well-reasoned case that international law required us to permit the PLO to continue its operations here. He cited precedents. He cited case authorities including an actual case captioned "The Good Ship Mazel Tov." He was overpowering.

Now it was my turn. I couldn't compete with Abe's scholarship if I tried. On three separate occasions I've heard Colin Powell tell the story of what took place next. He says I opened by saying, "Abe, your argument is as thin as a homeopathic soup made by boiling the shadow of a half-starved pigeon." According to Powell, that opening so dazzled and amused those assembled that the force of Abe's presentation was completely attenuated. As Powell tells it, the sentence I opened with was original with me. Not so. What he forgot was that I attributed the comment, and correctly so, to Abraham Lincoln who used it in a well-known debate with Steven Douglas. Epilogue: The decision was taken to close down the PLO in Washington and New York. I assigned the Washington case to the

United States Attorney in the District of Columbia. I assigned the New York case to Rudy Giuliani, then United States Attorney in the Southern District of New York. We won the Washington case. *I was right.* We lost the New York case, the court holding that the PLO had official status at the United Nations and, therefore, was entitled under applicable international law to maintain an office in New York City. *Abe was right.* Post-Epilogue: Years later, when Rudy was Mayor of New York City, Yasir Arafat, head of the PLO, during a week of meetings at the United Nations, showed up at Lincoln Center for a concert. The Mayor of New York had him thrown out of the theater. *Rudy was right.*

In the fall of 2004, Rudy Giuliani was the principal speaker at a gala fund-raising dinner held for the benefit of the Rabin Medical Center in Israel. My dear friend Abraham E. ("Barry") Cohen serves as chairman of the American Friends of the Center. Larry King conducted the evening festivities as master of ceremonies. I was asked to introduce Rudy Giuliani.

Obviously, this was essentially a Jewish crowd. On Passover, Jews all over the world participate in seders at which the Jewish exodus from Egypt—from slavery under pharaoh to freedom under Moses' leadership—is recounted as it is recorded in the written word of the Haggadah. The Haggadah contains a passage referred to as "Dayenu" (meaning it would have been sufficient) which is recited to thank God for all the blessings he conferred upon the Israelites. It starts like this:

> Had He brought us out of Egypt and not fed us in the desert, DAYENU!
>
> Had He fed us with manna, and not ordained the Sabbath, DAYENU!
>
> Had he ordained the Sabbath, and not brought us to Mount Sinai, DAYANU!

It goes on. You get the picture.

When I got up to introduce Rudy, I used the litany of the Haggadah to extol his virtues:

> Had he only been a fine lawyer and a leader of the New York Bar in his younger Days, DAYENU! It would have been sufficient.
>
> Had he only distinguished himself, as Associate Attorney General of the United States, one of the highest offices in the United States Department of Justice, DAYENU! It would have been sufficient.

Had he only been one of the finest and most successful United States Attorneys in United States history, I know, I was there, DAYENU! It would have been sufficient.

Had he only been the two term Mayor of New York City, who brought accountability, who brought fiscal reform to government, who reduced crime by 65%, who was responsible for New York City being named the safest large city in America, and who was responsible for the renaissance of the City of New York and the uplifting of the quality of life in our great city, DAYENU! It would have been sufficient.

Had he only rushed to the scene of the 911 attacks, placed himself in harm's way and successfully led the recovery of our City, as it faced its darkest hour, DAYENU! It would have been sufficient.

Had he only founded Giuliani Partners, a very successful full services firm, now in investment banking and proved himself as a very successful businessman, DAYENU! It would have been sufficient.

Had he only been a great friend of Israel, standing by her side, during one of her most difficult times, spreading encouragement to Israelis and Americans with both word and deed. DAYENU!

I remember. Do you remember?

The night Mayor Giuliani had a gun toting ruthless terrorist thrown out of Lincoln Center. His name was Yasir Arifat.

I remember. Do you remember?

. . .When he rejected a multi-million dollar gift from a Saudi Prince and told him to stuff It! DAYENU!

For all of his accomplishments and for all his personal attributes, we admire him and respect him. We appreciate him. Ladies and gentleman, Rudy Giuliani.

Following Rudy's speech which was extraordinarily well delivered and equally well received, Larry King "interviewed" him. Larry asked him how he could possibly hope to be the Republican candidate for President of the United States in 2008 when he was at odds with the people who control his political party on practically every social issue. Rudy's answer was interesting. He said that Larry's question brought to mind a conversation he had with Arnie Burns when he was first thinking of running for Mayor of New York City. Everyone told him that he could not possibly win the Mayoralty as a Republican because there were six Democratic votes for every Republican vote in the City of New York. And he was told that if by some miracle he did win, the Mayoralty is a political dead end. Rudy said that Arnie thought the opinions he was hearing were all wet and counseled him to go for it. Rudy concluded his answer to Larry's question by saying "and the rest is history."

When I am asked whether I think Rudy can become the Republican standard bearer in 2008, I respond that, in my view, his chances are directly proportional to the amount of anthrax in the air the day the decision is made.

CHAPTER 4

The Humor and Impact of Ronald Reagan

When an American Air Force plane shot down two Libyan jets, the White House was engulfed in controversy because aides failed to wake the President in the middle of the night. The next day, President Reagan got off a trademark quip: "I've laid down the law to everyone from now on about anything that happens, that no matter what time it is, I'm to be awakened, even if it's in the middle of a cabinet meeting."

Ronald Reagan, the fortieth President of the United States, was elected in 1980. He was the first president since our thirty-fourth President, Dwight D. Eisenhower, to serve two full terms. Kennedy, Johnson, Nixon, Ford, Carter all left office under less than desirable circumstances. President Kennedy was assassinated. President Johnson, mired in Vietnam, chose not to run again. President Nixon resigned. Presidents Ford and Carter, sitting presidents, each lost reelection. Ronald Reagan began his first term as a popular president and finished his second as a popular president. Few doubt that if not for the constitutional prohibition against a third term, if he had chosen to run again, he could have, and indeed would have, been elected for a third time.

As Deputy Attorney General, I attended a number of cabinet meetings, sitting in for the Attorney General when he was away from Washington. I often attended meetings of the Economic Policy Council and the National Security Council. I went to many meetings at the White House. In this way, I had the opportunity to see Ronald Reagan first hand. I also saw him at many public gatherings.

At the time I considered it a great privilege to have served with him. I still feel that way—even more so.

Ronald Reagan clearly viewed himself as an ordinary citizen who wound up in politics—not as a professional politician who pursued politics as a career. As Ed

Meese has said, Ronald Reagan genuinely believed that he did not seek politics but that politics had sought him. When you were with him, you had the distinct feeling that he was a man very comfortable in his own skin. He was not out to prove anything—not out for personal aggrandizement. He seemed to genuinely love to interact with people (a trait I later saw in President Bill Clinton). At the end of a meeting his aides would be tugging at him to go to the next scheduled event, say, a meeting with the King of Jordan or with the chancellor of Germany or the president of Turkey. He'd prefer to linger in conversation with the folks he was then with.

He came across as a regular guy—not at all an imperial or imperious president—not at all stuck on himself. He was frequently referred to as the great communicator. Absolutely right. If you were in a room with 500 other people and he addressed the group, you *knew* he was directing his remarks solely to you and that the other folks in the room were merely tag-a-longs. Each of the other 499 people felt exactly the same way.

He came to the presidency with an unusual mix of experience—a cavalry reserve officer before World War II, a radio sportscaster, a Hollywood actor, a maker of training films for the Air Force during the war, head of the Screen Actor's Guild (a union where he honed his negotiating skills) and two-term governor of California, in many ways a microcosm of the United States with—roughly 10 percent of the population and 10 percent of gross national product. If California were a country, its economy would rank as the fifth largest in the world.

How will Ronald Reagan go down in history? Only time will tell. But my guess is that Ronald Reagan will go down in history as one of our *great* presidents. Why do I say that? The big picture—future historians, in my view, will be influenced by three major points: (1) the death of communism (I have been all through eastern Europe during the last many years and, no doubt about it, he is credited with the downfall of communism); (2) the end of the threat of an Armageddon—nuclear war between the United States and the Soviet Union; and (3) a surge in economic prosperity.

In my book, Ronald Reagan did a superb job as a skilled political leader, as chief executive of the massive business of the federal government, as chief of state representing us in our relationships with other nations and their heads of state and as commander-in-chief seeking "peace through strength," both military and economic strength.

One cannot speak of Ronald Reagan without mentioning his sense of humor—a key part of his personality. At cabinet meetings I attended, he would open the proceedings with a current joke. He was a great raconteur. He was a master at using humor to relieve tension and to break the ice in dealing with people.

In her book, *When Character Was King*, Peggy Noonan puts it this way:

> Reagan sometimes used humor as a matter of courtesy. He knew people enjoyed laughing and he liked to give them little gifts—that's what his jokes were sometimes. Sometimes he used humor to make people who were nervous in his presence feel more confident. Sometimes he used it because he knew a gust of laughter gave people a chance to get their nervousness out. Sometimes he used it to get his own nervousness out, which is why he liked to begin his speeches with jokes.

Wearing my hat as Chairman of the Board of Governor's of Boys & Girls Clubs of America, I frequently told a story I first heard told by Ronald Reagan. I explain that if you give a dollar to Boys & Girls Clubs, 90 cents of it goes to programs for kids.

The story:

> There was this little boy who wanted to buy himself a wonderful set of trains which he saw in the window of FAO Schwartz in New York City and which cost $100. So he wrote a letter to God praying for him to send him $100 so he could make his very coveted purchase. The letter was seen and opened by the postmaster, who was very moved by the contents, so he decided to send it to President Reagan. Somehow it reached the President and when he read it, he too was moved by the little boy's plea. The President reached into his pocket and pulled out a $10 bill. He turned to one of his subordinates and said, "Send this boy this $10." When the boy received it, he wrote another letter to God, which by pure coincidence was again read by the postmaster and in turn sent to and read by the President, and it said, "God, thank you very much for sending me the money for the trains. Unfortunately, it was routed through Washington, D.C., and the bastards took out their 90%!"

I have often spoken about preparing our youngsters for challenging and fulfilling jobs and careers. I use a story I first heard told by President Reagan, in January 1988, when presenting the Presidential Rank Awards to members of the senior executive service at the White House. He told the story of the man who was out desperately looking for work. He pounded the pavements. He answered advertisements. He networked with friends and acquaintances. All to no avail. Finally, in desperation, he applied for a job at the local zoo. He was told that there would in due course be a permanent job there for him, but in the interim they wanted him on a temporary basis to do a special job. It seems as though their prize gorilla unexpectedly died. The temporary job was to don a gorilla suit and to work in the gorilla's cage until a new gorilla, on order, arrived. He put on the suit, got into the cage and after several days, he was really beginning to enjoy his work, cavorting for the children. He did somersaults. He did cartwheels. He swung on the rubber tire.

One day he became so exuberant while swinging on the big tire, he swung very high, lost his grip and soared through the air into the adjoining cage occupied by a ferocious lion. He had a fright. The lion charged at him, jumped him and roared. He started screaming blue murder. The lion turned to him and said, "For God's sake, shut up! You'll get us both fired!"

President Reagan also told this story:

> This fellow is driving west on the New Jersey Turnpike doing about 55 miles per hour when he spots in his rearview mirror a three-legged chicken gaining on him. Before he knows it, that chicken passes him doing about 65 miles an hour. He presses his foot down on the accelerator and he passes that chicken doing about 72 miles per hour. By God, before he knows it, he looks in his rearview mirror and that chicken passes him doing about 78 miles an hour. Down goes his foot on the accelerator again, but before he can pass that chicken, the chicken exits the next ramp. His curiosity is piqued so he follows him right off. The chicken turns off on a side road and pulls into a driveway of a farm house. This fellow follows him and screeches to a halt behind him. He is met by a farmer—the proprietor of the place—and he says to him, "My God, did you see that three-legged chicken?" The farmer says, "Yes, I breed them. People really like drumsticks and by having a chicken with three legs, it maximizes the value of the chickens." The fellow says, "Tell me, how do they taste?" The farmer says, "I don't know. Never been able to catch one!"

This is a lulu he used for Republican crowds:

> I remember once there was a fellow who was running for office, and he was in a rural area that wasn't known to be Republican. And he stopped by a farm to do some campaigning. And when the farmer heard he was a Republican, his jaw dropped and he said, "Wait right here while I go get Ma. She's never seen a Republican before." So he got her, brought her round, and the candidate looked around for a podium from which to give his speech, and the only thing he could find was a pile of manure. So he got up on that mound, and they gathered in front and he gave his speech. And at the end of it the farmer said, "That's

> the first time I ever heard a Republican speech!" And, the candidate said, "That's the first time I've ever given a Republican speech on a Democratic platform."

I never heard Ronald Reagan tell this one, but it's one of my favorite political jokes. I've used it often. The Southern farmer was introducing his family of boys to a visiting governor. "Seventeen boys," explained the governor. "And, all Democrats, I suppose."

"All but one," said the farmer rather proudly. "They're all Democrats but John, the little rascal. He got to readin!"

On March 30th, 1981, only nine weeks after he took office, the President was shot by John Hinckley. The President was rushed to the hospital and underwent surgery. When he opened his eyes in the recovery room, the first thing he said to Nancy was, "Honey. I forgot to duck."

When he was told he was going to be operated on, he looked up at the doctors and said, I just hope you're all Republicans."

When his top staffer came to visit in the late afternoon, he'd ask, "Who's minding the store?" When he was told the government was running OK, he asked, "What makes you think that news would make me feel better?"

President Reagan was often criticized for being lazy or not sufficiently involved. He deflected all this with good humor. In her book, *When Character Was King*, Peggy Noonan tells us President Reagan said, "I know hard work never killed anyone, but I figure, why take a chance?" And when reporters asked the President's staff how hard he was working, he would tell them to tell all of them he was really "burning the midday oil!"

On September 9th, 1987, President Reagan told the following story:

> This fellow is driving along an interstate highway and he is pulled over by a state trooper. He says, "What seems to be the matter officer? I don't think I was speeding." The policeman says, "No, sir, you were driving without tail lights." With that the fellow jumps out of the car, runs to the rear of the car, turns ashen white and becomes terribly, terribly agitated.
>
> The policeman says, "Sir, please don't get excited. This is not a serious infraction. It is nothing to be worried about." The driver turns to the policeman and says, "You may not be worried, but it appears as though I have lost my trailer and my wife and four kids!"

My wife Felice and I were privileged to attend the opening of the Reagan Presidential Library in Simi Valley, California. It was a fabulous day. All of the then living former presidents were in attendance. President Reagan spoke to a large group, a medium-sized group and, again, to a small group of us. At a small luncheon party for Mrs. Reagan here in New York over a year later, I mentioned this to her and told her it reminded me of the story about Sir Charles Chaplin who entered a Charlie Chaplin look-alike contest and came in second. I told her Ronald Reagan at Simi Valley was more like Ronald Reagan than anyone could be and in a Ronald Reagan look-alike contest he would have won hands down.

For me, it was a special honor to feel first hand the warmth of President Reagan's personality, to share his humor, to witness his genuine patriotism, and to see him at work with his theology of government as his core, sincerely charting what he believed was the correct course of action.

He was one of a kind. He was special. No doubt he greatly impacted America and the world during his time on our national stage.

CHAPTER 5

More Politics

Bush (41), Clinton and Bush (43)

Months after leaving the White House at the conclusion of his term as thirty-fourth President, Dwight Eisenhower was asked if leaving the White House had affected his golf game.

"Yes, he replied, "a lot more people beat me now!"

I first met George H.W. Bush in 1979. He was running for the Republican nomination for President of the United States. I was an ardent supporter. I made, for me, a substantial financial contribution to his campaign for which I received a small gold colored rectangular lapel pin with the candidate's name on it. I have it in my jewelry box to this day. In my opinion, no man was better trained by experience for that job than George Bush. He was a *bona fide* World War II hero, member of Congress, envoy to China, head of the CIA and United States representative to the United Nations, among other distinctions. And his opponent Ronald Reagan, in my opinion at the time, was, after all, only an actor. It did not take long for me to realize that my opinion of Ronald Reagan was all wet.

Over the years, I have had many occasions to spend time with George H.W. Bush:

- Felice and I were on two occasions invited to the official residence of the Vice President at the United States Naval Observatory in Washington, D.C.;
- He and I had a long visit with the widow and young daughter of DEA agent Enrique "Kiki" Camarena who was murdered in Mexico;
- I visited with him in his office when he was Vice President;
- He and Mrs. Bush came to New York to assist Rudy Giuliani in his campaign for Mayor and I, as chairman of Rudy's campaign, had the opportunity to spend some time with them;

- After he became President, I sent him a great book of photography taken during the Gulf War by the foremost photographers of the day. When sometime later, I was invited to the family living quarters in the White House, I was tickled pink to see the book I had sent the President on one of their tables;
- I had the privilege of meeting President Bush in the Oval Office on many occasions. I was with him very early in the morning when, late in the campaign, he was leaving the White House in the Presidential helicopter to beat the bushes for votes. He did not have an entourage. He seemed to me very much alone. After the election, which he lost to Bill Clinton, but before Clinton's inauguration, I saw him in the White House again. He seemed in a daze—stunned—as if he could not believe he had actually lost the election. I am pleased to see that George Bush and Bill Clinton have become good friends;
- When I was considering resigning from my job as Deputy Attorney General, I kept the Vice President, who was then running for President, fully informed through an intermediary—my Boys and Girls Club colleague, Robbie Callaway. Ed Meese resigned the Attorney Generalship after Bill Weld and I and our deputies left the Department. It was later reported to me that President Bush credited us with taking the "sleaze" issue out of the campaign to Bush's great advantage.

Over the years, I have had my photograph taken with George Bush many, many times. I treasure these photos.

Hanging on the wall in our apartment are two photographs taken on different occasions. Each of them depicts the then five living Presidents of the United States: George H.W. Bush, Ronald Reagan, Jimmy Carter, Gerald Ford and Richard Nixon. And each photograph contains the signature of each of them. It was not easy to put this together—almost impossible. There were four Republicans and one Democrat. I, of course, knew Presidents Bush and Reagan. Through friends and networking, I got the rest. I managed to get the signature of Richard Nixon with the help of my friend Ron Walker, who served in the Nixon administration, who was very close to the ex-President, and who, as a matter of fact, later handled all the funeral arrangements at the time of Nixon's death. I got President Ford's signature, but Jimmy Carter's was elusive.

One day I was on the shuttle from Washington, D.C. to LaGuardia. I was in the front row. Sitting next to me was an attractive woman. She looked familiar. Was she a movie star? A television personality? Someone I had met in business? Suddenly, it came to me. I was sitting next to Rosalynn Carter, the former first lady. I told her about my photograph signed by each of the Presidents except her husband. She volunteered to help. I sent her the photograph, he signed it, and she mailed it back to me.

I had the same problem with the second photograph. I managed by hook or by crook to get the Republicans. Again, I had no way of getting to Carter. That is until Boys and Girls Clubs of America moved its headquarters from New York City to Atlanta, Georgia, in 1994. Present at the ribbon cutting ceremonies was the Chief of Police of Atlanta. I seized upon the opportunity and maneuvered the chief into "volunteering" to get President Carter's signature for me. And by God, he did it.

I have had the privilege of spending time in the oval office with four presidents: George W. Bush, William Jefferson Clinton, George H.W. Bush and Ronald Reagan. During my time with the Reagan administration, I got to the White House with some frequency. To me, the White House is a national shrine. I never stopped being in awe of it. I never became jaded. Never took a visit there for granted.

Every year, Boys and Girls Clubs of America conducts a national contest to select its Youth of the Year. Finalists from five regions of the country compete for the honor. A week of exciting, eye-opening, activities in Washington, D.C. culminates with a visit, in the Oval Office, with the President of the United States. I was with the five youngsters on two occasions when they visited with George W. Bush. He was genuinely interested in them. He took significant time to explain the history of the oval office. He told them about the President's desk which had been presented to the United States by Queen Victoria. He talked about some of the artwork in the room. He explained that each President when he takes office gets to design a new office carpet. He delivered a little lesson on the economy. Clear, understandable, educational. He did not talk down to them. Photographs were taken. He could not have been more generous with his time.

Speaking of photographs, I remember vividly being in the oval office with President Reagan and the then Youth of the Year finalists. When we lined up for a photograph, President Reagan told the kids that when he first arrived in Hollywood, whenever a photo was being taken he would try to be dead center in the picture. He said that an old-timer told him to always be at the right end (facing the camera) i.e. on the left end (camera facing you) of the first row. That way, when the picture hit the newspaper or magazine the names of the persons in the photo are written from left to right. As a consequence, your name is the first one listed.

I first met George W. Bush at a meeting of major league baseball owners. He was then the principal owner of the Texas Rangers. I was there with my client George Steinbrenner. Bush is a regular guy. But in all honesty no one in the room that day would have ever imagined that he would one day be elected and re-elected President.

It is, of course, way too early to assess George W's Presidency. Suffice it to say that he presides during exciting and dangerous times. There is never a dull moment. And he has the courage, conviction and competence to handle the job.

I first met Bill Clinton, 42nd President of the United States, in December 1992. He had beaten President George H.W. Bush in the November election and was due to be inaugurated within weeks. Felice and I were invited to the Renaissance Weekend that year which was held in Hilton Head, South Carolina. Phil Lader, who later became the United States Ambassador to the Court of St. James, together with his wife, orchestrated the entire Renaissance Weekend concept of bringing together prominent folks from government, industry, the professions, the media, academe and diverse walks of life for candid discussions on the issues of the day. President elect Clinton and his wife Hillary Rodham Clinton were both in attendance.

I literally bumped into Bill in the hall one day. I introduced myself. He, surprisingly, knew who I was. I took the occasion to give him some advice about the Department of Justice. I had a lot to say to him but my message boiled down to urging him to depoliticize the Department. He seemed very interested in what I had to say. He told me that the Attorney General designate Zoe Baird (who, incidentally, did not become A.G. because of a nanny problem) was in Hilton Head and that he was anxious to have me talk with her. He told me that he would have her get in touch with me so that I could share my views with her. As someone who had a lot of experience with politicians, I knew to a certainty that I would never hear from either of them again. To my astonishment, the next day Zoe Baird found me. She said "Bill" wanted us to talk. So I invited Zoe to join me and my wife Felice for lunch. I repeated what I had already said to Bill Clinton, namely that the Department should be apolitical to the fullest extent possible and that it should concentrate on the even handed administration of justice. She seemed impressed. I knew to a certainty that I would never hear from either of them again.

On Saturday night the proceedings culminated in a dinner at which the President-elect was the keynote speaker. He was at the podium situated on a large stage ready to address the crowd. Felice and I were sitting in the audience close to the stage. Bill spotted me. He walked off the stage, came to our table and said to me "Arnie, did Zoe Baird follow up and meet with you?" I was stunned. I couldn't believe it. I assured him that she had and that we had had a good talk.

Hillary Clinton also spoke at the Renaissance gathering. She spoke without a note. It was my first encounter with her. It was clear that she was knowledgeable, brilliant, informed, politically savvy, magnetic and charismatic. Over the years, I have met her briefly on a number of occasions. Each time my impressions on our first meeting in South Carolina were reinforced.

Everything I have said about Hillary applied to Bill in spades. In addition, he genuinely loved people. He liked to engage people one on one. He connected with people big time. In this regard, he was very much like Ronald Reagan.

When my friend Louis Freeh was sworn in as Director of the FBI, another friend, Bill Fugazy and I attended the ceremony held in the courtyard of the

FBI building on Pennsylvania Avenue in Washington, D.C. President Clinton came and spoke. On his way out, he stopped to chat with Bill Fugazy who had sent the President a new golf club. Notwithstanding that his aides were pressing him to keep another appointment, he lingered. He and Fugazy spoke for a good 10 minutes about golf in general and the club in particular. He was in no hurry to leave. Years later, Fugazy was convicted of bankruptcy fraud, the prosecution having grown out of a knock down drag out fight Fugazy had with John Kluge, one of the richest men in America. Just before departing the Presidency, President Bill Clinton pardoned a host of convicted felons, including Bill Fugazy.

Unfortunately, according to Louie Freeh's account in his book about his tenure as Director of the FBI, his relationship with President Clinton, his boss, could not have been worse. They had virtually no contact with one another due principally to the fact that the President was mired in allegations of misconduct and wrongdoing. Notwithstanding, President Clinton enjoyed enormous popularity and, in my view, had he not been barred by a constitutional prohibition against another term, he would have, if he had chosen to run, been reelected to a third term.

During Clinton's presidency, on the recommendation of my long-time friend Allan Tessler, I served as the Second Circuit Representative on the American Bar Association Committee on the Federal Judiciary. The committee's role was to conduct extensive investigations of candidates for the Federal bench after the President had appointed them but before confirmation by the United States Senate. The idea was to interview the candidate and to speak with his or her colleagues, teachers, professors, employers, judges, adversaries, friends, foes, neighbors, etc. and then to assess the candidate's competence and temperament and to formulate a judgment to be shared with the nation as to whether, in the committee's opinion, the candidate was qualified, well qualified or not qualified to sit as a federal judge.

One of my tasks was to conduct the investigation of folks in the Second Circuit who knew Ruth Bader Ginsberg, "Kiki" Bader, as she was known then, was in my wife's undergraduate class at Cornell University. She was an attractive blonde at Cornell. As I think back on my investigation, two things stand out. First, I remember talking with one of her law professors at Columbia Law School. I've forgotten his name. During the course of our lengthy conversation, he told me that, in his view, Ruth Ginsberg was the most qualified person in the United States to join the Supreme Court. We talked further and he volunteered that he had said something earlier that was not quite correct. He said that Ruth Ginsberg was not the most qualified person. She was the second most qualified person. I naturally asked him who he thought was the most qualified. He responded by saying "Martin Ginsberg her husband" who incidentally is reputed to be one of the most brilliant tax lawyers in the country.

The second thing I remember is that the professor told me Ruth Ginsberg, because she was a woman, had great difficulty in getting a good law job in the private sector. He told me that early on in her career, she went to Sweden. She learned the Swedish language from scratch. She wrote the definitive text on Swedish procedural law in Swedish which was still in use at the time of my conversation with the professor.

Another one of the many tasks which fell to me as a member of the Bar Committee was to conduct the background investigation on Guido Calabrese, the former dean of the Yale Law School. Bill Clinton had appointed him to the United States Court of Appeals for the Second Circuit. Guido and I met in my office. We hit it off immediately and became and have remained friends. I learned during our chat that his father and mother were both Jewish. On his mother's side, he traced back to the Middle Ages Finzi Contini family, about whom a motion picture with the title "The Garden of the Finzi Contini" was made. His father was a distinguished physician in Italy. His father did not like Mussolini or his politics or his methods and Mussolini did not like him or his friends to put it mildly. So he packed up and left Italy with his family. They settled in Brooklyn, New York, without any source of income. When things looked very bleak, Guido's father received an appointment to the faculty of the Yale Medical School. When Guido's father died, he was buried in a Jewish Cemetery with Jewish ritual. Guido is a member of the Catholic faith. His wife is descended from John Jacob Audubon.

It goes without saying that Guido passed muster. And he has served with great distinction as a member of his prestigious court. Guido is brilliant and of a liberal bent. His nephew Steve Calabrese worked with me in the Department of Justice. He is also brilliant and of a decidedly conservative bent.

April 21st 1998. At the White House with President Reagan, Vice President Bush, et al, describing the malaise at Justice and explaining my decision to resign as Deputy Attorney General.

A sample of the cartoons which appeared all over the country depicting Attorney General Ed Meese as an Alice in Wonderland character—based on my ad lib remarks in testimony before the United States Senate on July 26, 1988.

My Wife Felice and I attended the opening of the Reagan Presidential Library in Simi Valley, California, on November 4th, 1991. Pictured on this historic occasion were the five living former Presidents (left to right): Bush, Reagan, Carter, Ford and Nixon.

President Reagan and me in the Roosevelt Room of the White House.

In Atlanta, Georgia, with my son Doug on the occasion of my presentation to President Carter of the Herbert Hoover Humanitarian Award, the highest honor bestowed by Boys and Girls Club of America.

President Bill Clinton and me in the Oval Office.

To Arnold Burns
With Best Wishes,

President George W. Bush and me in the Oval Office.

In the Oval Office with President George H.W. Bush as he signs the Simi Valley photograph of the five living Presidents.

Then Vice President George H.W. Bush and me in his office.

The 41st and 43rd Presidents of the United States inscribed by both to me.

Father and son inscribed by both to me.

Father and son fishing for stripers.

General Colin Powell and me.

My granddaughter Leah with Mayor Rudy Giuliani at Yankee Stadium.

Felice and me with Mayor Rudy Giuliani at Gracie Mansion.

CHAPTER 6

College Life with Humor

Robert Maynard Hutchins said a college president is one who must solve three problems: sex, for the students; football, for the alumni; and parking, for the faculty.

During a commencement address, Dr. William E. Moran, President of Colorado State University, said:

"Almost nobody listens to a commencement speech except, perhaps, a few parents engaged in one last effort to get something for their money."

Several college presidents were chatting about what they would like to do after retirement.

"Well," said one of them, "I know what I'd like to do. I'd like to be superintendent of an orphan asylum so I'd never get any letters from parents."

"I've a much better ambition," exclaimed another. "I want to be warden of a penitentiary. The alumni never come back to visit!"

Friend: "So, your son had to leave college on account of poor eyesight?"

College parent: "Yes, he mistook the dean of women for a co-ed."

Spring 1946. On April 14th, 1946, I celebrated my sixteenth birthday. I was a junior at Lynbrook High School in Lynbrook, New York, scheduled to graduate in June 1947. One problem. I was thoroughly bored at school and simply not intellectually challenged. I hatched a plan.

I concocted a cock and bull story and told my principal, Michael Brennan, that our family was moving to Pennsylvania. I said I coveted a New York State Regents Diploma. I explained that I had sufficient credits to graduate in three instead of four years and would, therefore, liked to graduate from the high school in June of 1946—one year early. I suggested that I would take my fourth year of high school in Pennsylvania as a post-graduate.

Not bad. Unfortunately, I was wholly ignorant of the fact that "Mike" Brennan and my father, Herman Burns, were friends who sat together at weekly Lions Club luncheons. My father was a merchant, the proprietor of a retail jewelry store by the name of Clayton Jewelers, located in the heart of the business district on Lynbrook's "five corners." At the very next Lions Club get together, "Mike" Brennan told my father how sorry he was that he and the family were moving out of state. Needless to say, my father was nonplussed and incredulous. The two men put their heads together and realized that, while my methodology was inexcusable, it was in everyone's interest that I not be kept in high school any longer than necessary.

So, despite my fibbing, in June 1946 I was indeed graduated (In June 2004, 58 years later, I was privileged to deliver the commencement address at the Lynbrook High School graduation ceremonies, the first commencement speaker in the history of the school who was not a member of its faculty or administration). Following my graduation, on the advice of Mr. Brennan, I applied for admission to Union College, his *alma mater.*

My application was *rejected.*

I then did something impetuous. I picked myself up, went to Grand Central Station and took the train to Schenectady, New York. In my young life that was quite an adventure—the equivalent of my now leaving here and going to Moscow.

It was a beautiful day in late spring. The Union College campus was beautiful—and well manicured—the trees full of foliage, the grass very green, the flowers in bloom. Undergraduates—then only men—were walking about in garnet sweaters with big white block "U's" superimposed upon them. A lacrosse game was in progress on Library Field. The Nott Memorial, a large sixteen-sided building, dominated the campus. The Nott Memorial is a landmark preservation building named after Eliphalet Nott, the great educator who was President of Union College the day Abraham Lincoln was born and President on the day, April 14th, 1865, Lincoln was assassinated. He served for the all-time record of sixty-one years.

On the dome of the Nott Memorial was an inscription in Hebrew, considered a classical language when the Nott was constructed, which roughly translated says, "The work is long, the day is short, the rewards are great and the Master of the house presses." This means there is so much to learn, so little time to learn it, and God presses us to pursue learning with a sense of urgency.

Once on campus I made my way to the office of Carter Davidson, the President of Union College. When the president asked why I was there, bolstered by the beauty and exciting activity on campus, I replied: "I am here because I want to go to Union College. I've applied for admission and I've been turned down."

President Davidson said, "Well, that's it," to which I said: "No, no, I *really* want to go here."

The president thought for a moment, looked me over, looked at the paperwork on me and reconsidered. He must have thought I had a lot of "moxie" or maybe a little "chutzpah." In any event, he said that I could join Union's Class of 1950. I was in!

I thought of this experience many years later in January 1982 on the day I was installed as Chairman of the Board of Trustees of Union College.

I was elected to the College Board of Trustees in 1976. I have been a Trustee for thirty years. I did my undergraduate work at Union, graduating more than fifty-five years ago. Our daughter, Linda, was graduated from Union in 1975, our son Doug in 1979. So I was a Union College parent for eight years. I served as Chairman for four years—1982 through 1985.

As you can see, a good chunk of my life has been committed to Union College. There is a solid tradition—almost a mystical phenomenon—of children and grandchildren, generation after generation of legacies, as descendants are called, attending Union College. I remember so well when some years ago, at a ceremony on campus, Al Hill, class of 1946, presented the college with the diploma of his direct ancestor who was graduated from Union Class of '97—that's *1797*—the year of Union's first graduating class. Al told me that every generation of Hills since had attended Union. You can't blame me for hoping that one or more of my grandchildren, Brendan (now an undergraduate student at Cornell), Leah and Scott, will matriculate at Union.

When I first walked through Blue Gate of the college as a student in 1950, Union was in an exciting state of flux. World War II was over. Veterans were going to college, many on the GI Bill of Rights. Enrollment at Union went up almost overnight to 1,500, about *twice* that which it had ever been before. According to William Huntley, dean of the college at the time, "there was all the wonderful ferment that the somewhat older men brought to the campus."

During my freshman year I shared a room with three classmates. Two of them were seventeen years old. The third was more than twice my age. He did not spend a whole lot of time in the room because he was having a torrid love affair with a beautiful divorcee whose bed he shared in downtown Schenectady on a regular basis. I don't know whether Dean Huntley had this in mind when he spoke of the ferment brought by older men to the campus, but our older roommate regaled and titillated us with tales of his sexual prowess, sometimes in clinical detail. This was surely a part of our education!

The first fraternity in America, *Kappa Alpha* was founded at Union College in 1825. During my time as a student, there was a deep tradition of fraternity life. And notwithstanding the infusion of mature men—the returning veterans—into the college community, freshman hazing in connection with fraternity rushing was definitely in vogue.

During hell week, the freshman pledges seeking admission into fraternities were run ragged around the clock. During the week, I had been assigned the tasks of producing fifteen 1911 pennies (1911 being the year our fraternity, *Kappa Nu*, was founded); five horse hairs at least nineteen inches long (Freihofer's horse-drawn bakery wagons, beware); specified items of lingerie from the collections of specified females; the verbatim inscription on the tombstone of one Giuseppe Aldi, to be obtained from the local cemetery from midnight to dawn armed with no light other than a pack of matches; certain items of anatomy from the underside of a bull, etc. After a week of sleepless scavenging, the final assignment on which allegedly, one's admission to the fraternity absolutely depended, was delivered. In each instance, the assignment was designed to be impossible of accomplishment.

Each pledge was called before the entire fraternity membership, under klieg lights, and asked to demonstrate that his assignment had been fulfilled. Once failure had been acknowledged, a vote would be taken and the pledge would be "blackballed." The pledge would be advised that to avoid the indelible stigma of rejection he should go through with the rest of the evening. The party line would be that he decided of his own volition to pass up fraternity life. The "rest of the evening" consisted of a drive to the vicinity of Plattsburgh, New York. Once there, the pledge would be given 10 cents for carfare back to Schenectady and informed that the entire evening was a hoax and that he was warmly welcomed as a fraternity brother. What a joyous relief!

> *My impossible assignment was to obtain the signature of the Governor of the State of New York* ON THE SHELL OF A RAW EGG.

Remember, our New York governor, Thomas E. Dewey, was a national figure. In 1940, he unsuccessfully tried for the Republican nomination for President of the United States. The Republican nominee was Wendell Wilkie, a native of Indiana. In 1944 Dewey was the Republican standard bearer and ran unsuccessfully against Franklin D. Roosevelt who won an unprecedented fourth term. (Later, in 1948, Dewey would again be the Republican presidential candidate, losing to incumbent Harry Truman in so close a race that the morning after the election, in a huge headline, the front page of the *Chicago Tribune* declared Dewey the winner!)

Notwithstanding Dewey's imposing national stature, I, a sixteen-year-old stripling, too stupid to know better, took the bus from Schenectady to Albany and found my way to the State Capital Building and the outer office of the Governor of the State of New York.

"What can I do for you, son," boomed a 6'4", 220-pound state trooper with broad vertical stripes down his long trouser legs and hash marks and chevrons up and down his sleeves to the 5'11", 130-pounder quivering before him. "I'd like to see the governor, sir," I squeaked. "What is the nature of your business?" "I'm not at liberty to say," I responded, scarcely believing I had the audacity to follow to the tee the instructions for the mission I was on. "Please take a seat." I did so very gently, favoring my right side. I was seated and, looking around me, saw a bevy of visitors waiting to see Governor Dewey, all of whom looked very distinguished and *very* old (certainly in their 30's). One man sat immaculately attired in a dark Brooks Brothers suit and perfectly groomed with a well-trimmed Van Dyke beard. He had a very thin, shiny black attaché case in his lap.

After what seemed like an interminable wait (actually about five minutes) the trooper came out and, preferring me above all the other chair-warmers, said "Son, the Governor will see you now." Weak-kneed, and faint-hearted and somewhat bewildered by it all, I rose and walked through to meet the governor of my state, wondering whether my nerve would hold up, and if so, what to say and how to say it.

I was ushered into the Governor's office and the former presidential candidate and public figure familiar to me through photos and newsreels, magazines and books, gave me a friendly smile and asked what he could do for me. Reaching gingerly into the right pocket of my jacket, I produced my uncooked egg and awkwardly blurted out my request that he sign it. The Governor asked me my name, where I hailed from, what school I attended. Right then and there I violated the injunction of my soon-to-become fraternity brothers against revealing my school affiliation and spilled all. When he learned I was from Malverne, New York, he asked me if I knew a number of people whom he quickly named. I acknowledged that I had heard of these dignitaries and was sure my father knew them.

The Governor, after chatting amiably, cordially, easily and sympathetically, asked for the egg and, by God, he signed it!

I was feeling mighty good—a little cocky—when I was hauled before the entire fraternity. When asked to show that I had succeeded in my assigned task, I hemmed and hawed for a moment and then triumphantly produced my coveted egg. A vote was to be taken on my candidacy for admission. Someone volunteered to speak on my behalf. He said that Arnie Burns was a good kid, he meant well, and that he'd be OK. Someone else spoke against my candidacy. He delivered a lengthy and detailed bill of particulars—perhaps, more accurately, an indictment, citing my many failings, character flaws and lack of social grace. I was voted down. The president of the fraternity, who had been a major in the United States Army, insisted on a revote because of the severe consequences and implications of a "blackball." All part of the charade. A re-vote was taken. I was voted down again. Never mind that I delivered the egg. Plattsburgh for me.

That was the first time I met Governor Dewey but not the last. He was the principal speaker at my commencement exercises in June 1950, and I met him on the street in Ithaca, New York, in 1952 where we exchanged brief anonymous hellos when I was studying law at the Cornell Law School.

In 1957, after a 3½-year tour of duty in the United States Army as an advanced infantryman and then as an army lawyer, I decided to seek employment in New York. In the recesses of my mind lay my Albany excursion and, as a shot in the dark, I applied for a job with the prestigious New York law firm of which Governor Dewey was the senior partner, having retired from public life to become a leader at the bar. To my surprise and delight, one of his partners hired me. During my three-year tenure with the firm, I was to work as the Governor's assistant on important cases. I learned my trade at the elbow of a master craftsman—who became my mentor and friend. When I left his firm in 1960 with Stanley Lesser to form our own, thirteen years after the Albany visit, I reminded him of the incident and we enjoyed the reminiscence together.

Thus, a chance experience made an indelible imprint upon my life and permanently influenced the course of my professional career.

When I was a student you were not required to attend class if you were on the dean's list. No kidding. So long as you remained on the dean's list, you could cut as many classes as you wished. For some reason, I made a habit of not going to my German class. Finally, I simply had to show up. My classmates warned me that our German professor, Herr Hicks, was lying in wait ready to ambush me when I deigned to appear. I resolved to go to class. I learned that the assignment was to memorize the soliloquy from *Faust*—in German, of course. I boned up. I studied. I committed it to memory. I knew it cold. I came to class. Herr Hicks called on me to recite. With great confidence I faced the class. My mind went blank. I had a mental block. I froze. I had to sit down, totally embarrassed. Would you believe that I can today recite: "Habe nun ach philosophie, juristerei und medizin und leider auch teologie, etc. etc. etc."

That's how well I drummed it into my head over fifty-five years ago.

This brings to mind this little bit of whimsy:

> Voice on the phone: "John Smith is sick and can't attend classes today. He requested me to notify you."
>
> College professor: "All right. Who is this speaking?"
>
> Voice on the phone: "This is my roommate."

In 1978 my wife Felice and I loaned a collection of 48 contemporary graphic prints we had acquired and put together in the Herman and Rose Burns (my parents) Collection. I had all the prints suitably framed. The collection represented dominant trends in contemporary art in America and included work of such pivotal artists as Joseph Albers, Sam Francis, Roy Lichtenstein, Robert Motherwell, Robert Rauchenberg and Frank Stella.

We attended a luncheon at the Schenectady Museum where those works of art were on display. I was asked to say a few words. I told them that good friends of ours had twins who were born prematurely. The mother was discharged from the hospital in ordinary course. Her tiny twin girls had to remain in an incubator at the hospital until they were further developed. Three weeks after she left the hospital, and took up her former life, the mother received a phone call from the maternity ward advising her that she had to come by and pick up her infants. Her immediate and spontaneous reaction was to exclaim: "Can't you keep them for at least another week!"

I explained that Felice and I lived in constant fear that one day someone from the college would call us and ask us to pick up our prints. We absolutely had no room for them. To relieve our apprehension, I said, we then and there gifted the entire collection to the college.

I have on numerous occasions asked people who they thought was the greatest president of the United States. I have put the question over the years to my children and grandchildren. I remember one time standing in the East Wing of the White House before a huge portrait of this man and exclaiming to those gathered around me that he was, without question, the best president the United States ever had. The man—Chester A. Arthur, our twenty-first President. He was a graduate of Union College!

One other President of the United States attended Union College for post-graduate work in physics after he was graduated from the United States Naval Academy. His name—Jimmy Carter, our thirty-ninth President.

I attended the Democratic National Convention, convened in New York City, which nominated Jimmy Carter as the Democratic standard bearer. Why and how I got there I do not remember. After all, I am a card-carrying Republican. At any rate, I do remember that they had a huge screen on which they ran a biographical movie about Carter's life.

There was enormous emphasis on Carter's time as a student at Union College. The Georgia man needed a Northeast connection, and his experience as a Union graduate student provided it.

In 1976, the country celebrated the bicentennial of the signing of the Declaration of Independence. A china factory in Denmark was also celebrating its 200th anniversary. To commemorate both events, the Danish company created a magnificent coffee and tea set. On each piece—on the cups, on the coffee pot, on the teapot, on the sugar bowl, on the creamer and on the tray—were silhouettes of the founding fathers of our nation. It was exquisite. I couldn't resist. I bought it. I soon realized that this treasure should be shared with others. I gave it to the college.

During the Carter presidency, I invited Jimmy Carter to return to Union. I wanted to serve him coffee or tea using the commemorative china. Unfortunately, he could not accept the invitation. My son, Doug, and I, however did have the opportunity to chat with former President Carter about his days at Union College. At the latter part of 2002, I was privileged to present President Carter with the Herbert Hoover Humanitarian Award, the highest honor bestowed by Boys & Girls Clubs of America. All joking aside, President Carter is one of the best, arguably the very best, past president we ever had. This is because of his very tangible commitments to world peace, alleviating poverty and helping the needy around the world.

When I served as Chairman of the Board of Union, I was called on to speak at various college functions. I remember on one occasion making the point that the success of the college depended upon a true collaboration among administration, faculty and alumni. It was not a one-dimensional show. I used this story to help make the point:

> The musician was giving a brilliant concert in a famous old church. As he reached the intermission, he retired to the back of the organ for a bit of rest. There he found an oldish gentleman smoking his pipe as he rested from the chore of pumping air for the big organ. The fellow smiled and commented, "We're giving them quite a concert, aren't we?"
>
> This seemed out of perspective to the genius, who put the fellow in his place, "What do you mean, 'we,' old man? I'm giving the concert!"

> He went out front. In came the audience, he struck the pose with hands raised and let them descend for the next number. There was no sound. He dashed behind the organ. There was the man, smoking his pipe and continuing to rest. It dawned on the genius and with a smile he admitted, "You were right, *we* are giving them a concert."

When explaining that we were charting a new course—creating a new direction—for the college, I told the following baseball story:

> George Earnshaw, the well-known Philadelphia right-hander of yesteryear, was pitching for Connie Mack's Athletics against the New York Yankees on a day when the famed Bronx Bombers of old were in a deadly slugging mood. Before a couple of innings had been played, Big George Earnshaw had had more than his share of trouble for one baseball day.
>
> Among his chief tormentors was the late Lou Gehrig, who in his first two times at bat socked two home runs into the *right-field* stands. After the second homer, Manager Connie Mack lost his patience and yanked the faltering pitcher out of the game. Disgusted with himself, Earnshaw started for the clubhouse but Connie Mack sharply called him back to the dugout and ordered him to sit down. "You sit right here next to me for the rest of this game. I want you to watch how Mahaffey is going to pitch to that Gehrig fellow." Earnshaw plunked down on the bench, resigned to watch his successor hurl against the rampaging Yankees. Presently, up to bat again came Lou Gehrig, and this time he parked the first pitch into the *left-field* stands for another home run. There was a long and awkward silence finally broken by Earnshaw, who turned to his manager and said, "I see perfectly what you mean, Mr. Mack. He sure made Gehrig change direction."

In the 1980's, Felice and I funded the creation of the Herman and Rose Burns Atrium dedicated to the memory of my parents. The dedicatory plaque reads:

> Dedicated to the memory of Rose and
> Herman Burns who believed that education
> built on a solid foundation of moral values
> is the means of breaking all barriers to high
> achievement and a life of fulfillment.

CHAPTER 7

In-the-Army-Now Humor

A sergeant and a private were hauled before a general court martial for the very serious offense of striking a superior officer. Both of them socked a colonel. The sergeant took the stand in his own defense and explained, in extenuation and mitigation, that he had a very sore toe with a huge bunion on it, and during inspection the colonel walked by and stepped on his sore toe. Reflexively, he punched him. He expressed his contrition and his apologies. When the private took the stand in his own defense, he explained that when he saw the sergeant punch the colonel in the face, he figured the war was over. So he thought he would hit him too.

General Al Haig, former Secretary of State, at a gathering at Freedoms Foundation at Valley Forge, told the story of an American army aviator who was flying at all hours around the clock during the Berlin airlift. The Soviet Union had blocked all vehicular traffic into landlocked Berlin, a city totally surrounded by Soviet-controlled East Germany. On this particular occasion the American pilot was flying some members of Congress out of Tempelhof Airport, Berlin. He looked particularly haggard. A Senator, aware of the brutal schedule the pilots were keeping, sympathetically inquired of the pilot as to the last time he was in the company of a woman.

The pilot responded, "1945."

The Senator gasped and said, "My God, that's awful."

The pilot responded with, "That's not so terrible. It's only 2100 now."

On November 6th, 1953, I was inducted into the United States Army as a buck private.

Two days before, on November 4, I had become a lawyer. The investiture ceremony took place at the courthouse of the Appellate Division of the New York Supreme Court in Brooklyn, New York. Typically such an investiture involves a cast of hundreds—hundreds of new lawyers being sworn in. On this occasion, however, there were only two candidates for admission to the bar. I was one of them. I came dressed in a brand new dark blue striped suit, accompanied by my wife Felice, my parents, Felice's parents and my two sisters, Ruth and Norma. The other candidate was similarly attired. He, too, was surrounded by wife and family. The ceremony was short, sweet and dignified.

I quit my employment as a neophyte lawyer with a first-rate law firm and volunteered for the draft. The Korean War was still on. I took sixteen weeks of basic infantry training and then another sixteen weeks of advanced infantry training, during a mighty cold winter, at Fort Dix.

I arrived at Fort Dix, New Jersey, on November 6. Dressed in sloppy Army fatigues, I was going through the chow line at Fort Dix, with a steel tray in my hand. A blob of mashed potatoes was thrown on my tray. I looked up at the server. Imagine my surprise. It was none other than the lawyer I was sworn in with two days before. He was an old-timer. He was inducted one day ahead of me. What a change of circumstances! (More than 30 years later, when I served in the Justice Department, I was invited to the Pentagon to lunch with John Marsh, Secretary of the Army. Our agenda included a discussion of the "war on drugs" and the Army's very successful program which reduced drug use in the ranks. At one point in our conversation, I asked the Secretary a question for which he did not have an answer. He summoned the Chief of Staff of the United States Army, four star General John Wickham, who treated me as if I were really important yessiring me and nosiring me to beat the band. At that moment, I remembered so vividly my first day in the Army on the chow line with steel tray in hand.)

Remember, at that point I was a college graduate, a law school graduate and a member of the bar. The Army classification system, in its own inimitable way, decided that I should become (have you guessed it?) a COOK. I confess I have acquired certain culinary skills since then (my Sunday morning eggs ranchero and eggs Burns are superb!) but I had no such skills at the time. Somehow, I avoided going to cook school. Instead, I wound up in the 37th Armored Division at Fort Knox, Kentucky. After entering the Army, I applied for a commission with the Judge Advocate General's Corps, but this was a very highly competitive proposition and the chance of getting selected, in my mind, was practically nil.

Our JAG group was composed of very able young men. Members became Deans of the Harvard Law School, Georgetown Law School, Michigan Law School and Duke Law School. Two of them, Derek Bok and Ken Pye, went on to become President of Harvard University and Chancellor of Duke University, respectively. Others, of course went on to great careers as well.

Felice was able to accompany me to Fort Knox. I worked as a clerk in battalion headquarters for a good guy, a lieutenant colonel. One day, about ten months after my induction into the service, my boss, the colonel, asked me to go down to Company A headquarters and to bring back the Company "guide on" as it was going to be needed for a battalion parade. Post haste, I took myself down to Company A. I told the corporal behind the desk that I had come, at the colonel's direction, to get the Company "guide on." He looked at me quizzically. He seemed baffled. I explained, "I've come for the Company flag."

A young, red-cheeked second lieutenant, who hadn't started to shave yet and who obviously was a product of an ROTC college program, happened in at that moment. He turned to me and said, "We know damn well what a 'guide on' is soldier." I said, "OK." He told me to stand at attention when in the presence of an officer. I did so. He told me to address him as "Sir." "Yes, Sir." He inquired as to when I had last polished my shoes and my belt buckle. He dressed me down—but good. He embarrassed me. He humiliated me. Mercifully, I was finally released and with "guide on" in hand, returned to battalion headquarters. As I walked in the door, my boss got up, stood at attention and saluted ME. He told me that I was being commissioned a first lieutenant in JAG. My orders had just come through. He explained that his lieutenant colonelcy was a temporary rank and that his permanent rank was master sergeant. In that sense, he said, I was *his* superior officer. That's why he saluted me.

I was ordered to the separation center the next day for discharge as an enlisted man. The moment after I was discharged, I took the oath as an officer in the United States Army. I was posted to Fort Benning, Georgia, for infantry school where I'd learn to lead an infantry platoon in combat.

Felice and I packed all our worldly possessions, threw them into our Chevy, and were off to Fort Benning. I told Felice about the "guide on" incident. I explained that before we left the post, I was going back to Company A. I was going to call that S.O.B. second lieutenant on to the parade ground and I was going to excoriate him in front of the Company.

Felice told me very nicely and very wisely that this was a great test of character for me. If I called out the red-cheeked second "louie," I would vent my spleen and get some immediate petty gratification. The bigger, the better, the mature man would ignore this minor satrap and leave the post forthwith. That was the higher course. I followed her advice. AND I HAVE REGRETTED IT EVER SINCE AND HAVE NEVER FORGIVEN HER!

After Fort Benning, I was ordered to the University of Virginia in Charlottesville, the home of the Judge Advocate General's School. The Commandant was Colonel Charles Decker. He was an Army lawyer who had graduated from the United States Military Academy at West Point. He was a gentleman. He was a patrician. He was courtly. He was gracious. And he had a passion for American history. He taught one class, the subject of which was the early days of our Republic.

At each of our sessions, he'd stride into the room. The class would jump to attention. With a slight bow and a flourishing wave of the hand, he would say, "Take seats please, gentlemen."

One day in the middle of a lecture he turned to the class and posited a question. Who was the law teacher of the great Chief Justice John Marshall. "Lt. Givens." "I don't know, Sir." "Lt. Pines." "I don't know, Sir." "Lt. Smith." "I don't know, Sir." "Lt. Burns."

I had absolutely no clue as to the answer. So far as I knew I had never run into this arcane bit of trivia. But mystically, magically, inexplicably, I heard my own voice say, "Was it George Wythe, Sir?"

Bullseye! Colonel Decker was delighted. He and I bonded then and there.

After completion of our course at JAG school, I was posted to Washington, D.C., assigned to the Government Appellate Division. There I learned my craft. There I honed my skills. There I became a full-fledged lawyer.

I argued 40 reported cases before the United States Court of Military Appeals (reported in volumes 6, 7 and 8 of the USCMA reports and in volumes 20, 21, 22, and 23 of the CMR reports) and over 100 cases before lesser military tribunals, involving a whole gamut of crimes from murder to robbery to larceny to rape, and all kinds of peculiarly military offenses. What a rich experience!

The cases I argued before the Court of Military Appeals included important landmark cases involving the prosecution of our American soldiers who were interned in Chinese POW camps during the Korean War and subsequently charged with collaboration with the enemy. They attracted international attention:

United States v Batchelor—sentenced to twenty years for collaboration with the enemy, misconduct by informing on a fellow prisoner and wrongfully participating in the trial of a fellow prisoner in which he recommended that the other soldier be executed; *United States v Gallagher*_—sentenced to life imprisonment for two counts of unpremeditated murder of two fellow prisoners, collaboration with the enemy and three counts of mistreatment of fellow prisoners of war; and *United States v Fleming*—sentenced to dismissal from the service for collaboration with the enemy, leading discussion groups reflecting the opinion that the United States was an illegal aggressor and making for broadcast communist propaganda recordings designed to promote disloyalty of United States troops and praising the enemy and attacking the war crimes of the United States. Legal issues included the permissible extent under the Constitution of military jurisdiction over military personnel following a hiatus in military service (Gallagher); amnesty as a defense (Batchelor); good motives and the threat of non-immediate duress and coercion not a defense (Fleming).

In 1960 under the auspices of the Committee on Military Justice of the Association of the Bar of the City of New York, I, together with a good friend, Don Rapson, rewrote the Uniform Code of Military Justice, which was originally enacted in 1951. Our revisions of the Code were introduced in the Senate by Senator Jacob Javits and in the House by Representative John Lindsay. And they were duly enacted into law.

We proposed a number of significant reforms in military law. The most significant was to insure that the law officer, that is, the trial judge at a general court martial, was completely independent. Under the existing Uniform Code, the law officer was appointed by the commanding officer who actually referred criminal charges to a general court martial and ordered the court convened. Moreover, the law officer was usually under the command of the convening authority. So, the inherent defect in the system was that the law officer sitting as the trial judge in a general court martial was subject to command pressure from the very officer who ordered the case tried in the first place.

Our bill mandated that law officers, in a circuit riding system, would receive assignments solely from the Judge Advocate General and would be under his command. Thus, the law officer was insulated from command influence, in effect making him an independent judge.

I remember one case I argued before an army board of review. The accused was one, Sergeant Chavez, a Native American. Chavez and his wife, also a Native American, lived on the military post at Fort Jackson, South Carolina. One night a huge burley soldier broke into the home of a neighbor of the Chavez couple and crawled into bed with the woman of the household whose husband had drawn some night duty. He raped her.

Mrs. Chavez was frightened. She went to headquarters and asked that an M.P. be assigned to patrol her neighborhood. When that request was refused because of a dearth of police personnel, she asked for and got permission to keep a revolver for her own protection. She bought one. During the middle of one pay period, the couple's financial resources were low so they pawned the gun for some ready money. On payday, which coincided with the sergeant's birthday, the couple decided to go to the NCO (non-commissioned officer) club to celebrate. They took a yellow post taxi to the club and on the way detoured off-post to stop at the pawnshop and to redeem the revolver.

As they stepped out of the taxi when they arrived at the club the bullets fell out of the clip and wound up on the dusty ground at their feet. Chavez cleaned the bullets, put them back in the clip and, to avoid a repetition of dropping them, inserted the clip into the revolver.

Once inside, the couple settled into chairs at their own table and ordered glasses of beer. Along came a 6'4" soldier, also a Native American, who started to flick ashes into the sergeant's beer. Chavez said, "No sweat." The soldier persisted. He flicked again and a third time. Chavez, each time, said, "No sweat." The soldier then put his arm around Mrs. Chavez and fondled her breast. Mrs. Chavez stood up, grabbed a beer bottle and smashed it against the edge of the table, and brandishing her self-made lethal weapon said to the soldier, "Look I am a Cherokee and if you touch me one more time, I'll kill you." The soldier said, "You are a whore," and spat in her face.

Sergeant Chavez emptied the revolver into the soldier.

Chavez was tried by general court martial and was convicted of first degree murder. He was sentenced to life imprisonment. The commanding general, on the advice of his staff judge advocate, and in his infinite wisdom, reduced the sentence to thirty-five years.

The case was appealed to the Board of Review. I was the lawyer for the government. Citing case precedents, I argued that there was sufficient time between the firing of the first round and the firing of the last round for the accused to premeditate. Chavez' lawyer argued brilliantly. He pointed out that if it hadn't been for the rape, if it hadn't been for the lack of military police, if there had been no gun, if it hadn't been for the lack of finances and the need for the pawn, if it hadn't been for the dropping of the bullets on the sandy ground, if it hadn't been for the fact that the clip of bullets was inserted into the gun, the homicide would never have happened. The Board of Review did not buy my argument. They reduced the conviction to voluntary manslaughter and cut the sentence to ten years.

"Now," as Paul Harvey would say, "the rest of the story." One day, not long thereafter, I am sitting in my office on the fifth floor, E ring, of the Pentagon and I get a telephone call from The Judge Advocate General. TJAG wants to see me.

His name was Eugene Caffey. He was a Major General. He was TJAG. He was God. He hailed from Las Cruces, New Mexico, where men are "macho" and protect their women folk. I saluted. He turned to me and said, "Burns, what is this Chavez case all about?" I told him the whole story. I gave him the entire picture. He said, "Burns, what would you have done if this soldier had done that to *your* wife." I responded: "I would have killed the son of a bitch, Sir."

TJAG turned to me and said, "Burns, Chavez walks out of prison today."

In the late 1950's, I had occasion to visit Fort Jay on Governor's Island in the New York Harbor. It was a beautiful post. The Officers' Club was fabulous. On the evening I was there, a party for a retiring general was in progress. In his remarks, the honoree told about the old bull and the young bull who were grazing together at the bottom of a hill. The young bull exclaimed: "Look at all those heifers up there on that plateau. Let's run up the hill and screw one of those heifers." The old bull responded: "No, son, let's walk up that hill and screw all of those heifers!"

I can't resist sharing with you the story about four people riding in a train coach. A woman and her beautiful nineteen-year-old daughter are on one side, and facing them, are an army general and his escort, an army private. The train enters a tunnel, and the cabin becomes dark. A kiss is heard, followed by a slap. The mother thinks, "That young man stole a kiss from my daughter, and she rightfully slapped him." The daughter thinks, "That young man tried to kiss me and kissed my mother by mistake and got slapped." The general, cheek smarting, thinks, "That young man stole a kiss, and I got slapped by mistake." The private thinks, "I'm pretty smart. I kiss the back of my hand and get to hit the general."

Earlier, I mentioned Colonel Decker. He was promoted to Brigadier General and later to Major General. He became TJAG. He and I did some public speaking together, addressing some local Washington, D.C., civic groups. When my tour of duty came to its end, the general tried to persuade me to remain in the Army. I was flattered. It was tempting. Felice and I talked it over. We opted for a return to civilian life.

For my service as an army lawyer, I was awarded a medal, the Commendation Ribbon with Metal Pendant, popularly referred to as "the Green Hornet." I was honorably discharged as a Captain.

CHAPTER 8

JEWISH LAUGHTER

> *A fellow walks into a restaurant on the lower East Side of New York which specializes in Jewish-style cuisine. He is taken care of by a Chinese waiter who speaks to him in fluent Yiddish. As the patron leaves the restaurant, he pays his check and comments to the proprietor taking money at the cash register that it was extraordinary that the Chinese waiter spoke Yiddish so beautifully.*
>
> *The proprietor replies in hushed tones, "Shush! He thinks I'm teaching him English!"*

Judaism is 5,767 years old. Over the centuries—indeed, over millennia—Jewish communities have flourished and have died; have been welcomed and have been expelled; have been honored and have been ostracized; have waxed and have waned; and have flowed and have ebbed. When economic, political, military upheavals and other troubles surface, the going gets tough for Jews. They have been knocked about. They are and have been historical scapegoats. Inexplicable but true.

That is why we American Jews here in the 21st century are so damned lucky. Lucky to live in a free democracy. Lucky to live in a free market economy. Lucky to live under a written Constitution which protects the rights of all minorities. (We Americans hold the world's record for the longest time for a republic under a written constitution.) Lucky to have an independent judiciary. Lucky to have a government with power fractionated because of checks and balances. Lucky to have equal opportunity for all citizens.

I don't think we will ever succeed in eradicating anti-Semitism or bigotry in all its forms but we must be constantly vigilant and keep it in check. That's why we must support the Anti-Defamation League which has been fighting bigotry around the world since its founding in 1913. That's why we must support other worthwhile organizations engaged in battling prejudice.

I was brought up in Lynbrook, New York. I attended the public schools there. My father Herman Burns was born in Portland, Maine, in 1898. My mother, Rose, emigrated to the United States in her mother's arms from the Ukraine in 1904 when she was two years old. My parents, each in his and her own way, were loving, caring, nurturing and self-sacrificing. I had a happy childhood. I have often wondered whether there might be something wrong with me because in this modern introspective age I do not loathe, resent or have ambivalent feelings about my parents.

Lynbrook had a small Jewish community. There were two synagogues: Congregation Beth David (where I learned to drink hard whiskey and play pool) and Temple Emanuel (where Felice won the oratorical contest in her sixteenth year.) The synagogues produced two great rabbis: Rabbi Emanuel Rackman, who as I write this is Chancellor of Bar Elan University in Israel, and the late Rabbi Harold Saperstein. (Rabbi Saperstein married Felice and me; his grandfather married my grandparents in Portland, Maine.)

Pre-World War II, we had an active Ku Klux Klan in Lynbrook with occasional cross-burnings. The Catholic Church preached and taught anti-Semitism from their pulpits and parochial schools. The German American Bund was fully operative. I remember so well going to the home of a seventh grade friend and seeing a huge portrait of Adolph Hitler hanging over the fireplace mantel. One day a ninth grader from the high school across the street of German ancestry walked through our elementary school playground and yard simulating the wiping of his behind with a Jewish newspaper. A big seventh grader by the name of Katz took umbrage at this spectacle. A classic schoolyard fight took place. I was happy. The seventh grader beat the hell out of the ninth-grade bigot.

In this environment, Jewish kids were from time to time harassed and molested by gentile kids—but nothing too violent or too traumatic so far as I know.

Now, follow this exercise. Write down 5,767. Subtract 3,007. What does the answer mean? Simple. 5,767 is the current year in the Jewish calendar. 3,007 is the age of the Chinese nation and culture. When you do the subtraction, you get 2,760—the number of years Jews had to live and survive without Chinese food!!

When I concluded my second year of law school I went to work as a summer man at a prestigious law firm of about 25 lawyers, which was housed in a beautiful mahogany paneled office at 25 Broad Street in New York City. There were two lawyers there about ten years my senior who both had recently been elevated to partner status. They were both graduates of the Cornell Law School, my *alma mater*. They were tops. Tops as lawyers. Tops as mentors. They took me under their wings. They became my good friends.

As my tour of duty with Army JAG was coming to an end, I thought about this firm for permanent employment. I went for an interview. My two friends received me with open arms. They wanted me to work there. They were very encouraging. I was interviewed by the senior partner—the head man. Following that meeting, my two friends sat me down and broke the bad news. I was not going to get a job offer. The senior partner, they explained, did not think I was properly attired. The lapels on my suit were either too narrow or two wide, I don't remember which. The fact that I had been wearing an army uniform almost exclusively for 3½ years did not excuse my appearance. I was crestfallen. My ego shattered. I was embarrassed.

About twenty-five years later I was serving as head of the Cornell Law School capital campaign or annual fund, or both. I called one of my former mentors (the other one had ceased practicing law) to hit him up for a large donation. He had moved to a large and very distinguished law firm. He was delighted to hear from me and insisted on hosting me for lunch at his club. In those days, it was not that unusual to have a two-martini lunch. My host and I had a three-martini lunch. He took the occasion to tell me how very proud he was of me and of my accomplishments. He told me that I built and headed a fine law firm; that I had become a leader of the bar; and that I was an important member of our community. The third martini was beginning to kick in. He turned to me and inquired: "Do you remember when you came home from military service and were seeking a job with our firm?" I acknowledged that I surely did remember. He continued, "I'll never forgive those bastards—those partners of mine. The only reason they didn't hire you was because you were Jewish!"

What a revelation. If only they had told me the truth at the time. I could easily have handled their anti-Semitic decision. After all, I had run into that kind of prejudice before. But to tell a youngster that his clothes were improper. I consoled myself by thinking that Abe Lincoln could not have gotten a job there. I did something about it though. Ever since, I kept a wardrobe of over 20 suits.

During the evening following our three-martini luncheon, I told Felice what had transpired. She quickly repaired to my clothes closet. She picked out a half dozen suits to be immediately dispatched to the garbage heap!

We all know that the ability to properly identify persons is at times vitally and critically important. Here are two stories to make the point:

> Three Jewish women were walking along the beach outside their hotel in Miami Beach, Florida. Lying on the sand was a man with a newspaper completely covering his face obviously to protect him from a sunburn. Embarrassingly, his bathing trunks were askew and his private parts were completely exposed. The first woman remarked, "Well, thank God he's not my husband."

The second woman, peering over the first woman's shoulder, agreed, "You're right, he's not your husband."

The third woman, somewhat older than the other two, bent over to look and said, "*He's* not even a guest at our hotel."

Middle-aged Mrs. Cohen had a heart attack and was taken to the hospital. While on the operating table, she had a near death experience. Seeing God she asked, "Is my time up?"

God said, "No, you have another 43 years, 2 months and 8 days to live."

Upon recovery, the woman decided to stay in the hospital and have a facelift, liposuction and a tummy tuck. She even had someone come in and change her hair color. Since she had so much more time to live, she figured she might as well make the most of it.

After her last operation, she was released from the hospital. While crossing the street on her way home, she was killed by an ambulance. Arriving in front of God she demanded, "I thought you said I had another forty plus years? Why didn't you pull me out from the path of the ambulance?"

God replied, *"I didn't recognize you."*

Not long after I became a Trustee of Union College, the then president of the college asked me to call on a Union alumnus, Milton Canter. Canter lived in Washington, D.C. He was reputed to be quite wealthy. And he had never given a nickel to Union College.

In Washington on some legal matter before the Securities and Exchange Commission, I scheduled a visit with Canter. He was extremely cordial. He was a real gentleman of the old school. He turned to me and he said: "You say you are a Trustee of Union College? I take it you are Jewish." I acknowledged that I was. He finished with, "If you are Jewish, there is no way you can be a Trustee. Let me tell you a story."

He then went on to tell me about the time he applied for admission to the college. He came to the campus for a personal interview with "Dutchy" Barnes, the Dean of Admissions. After a pleasant enough chat, the dean turned to him and said, "Canter, you're a good boy with a fine record, but you can't come to Union. You are a Jew. We have a quota of 1 percent of the entering class for Jews. The quota is filled. We have no room for you."

Canter reacted by stating his keen disappointment. "Dutchy" Barnes peered at him. He said, "Canter, I like you. Where are you from?" "Poughkeepsie, sir." He thundered, "You're not from New York City?" "No, sir." "Canter, I like you. I'm going to make an exception in your case and accept you for admission."

I persuaded Canter that Union College had changed. That day, he wrote a check for $1,000 payable to the College. He became my law partner. Our firm opened a satellite office at 15th and M Streets. Canter was resident partner in charge. Walter Washington, who had been Mayor of Washington, D.C. for eleven years, joined us as a partner. Canter introduced me to the Boys & Girls Clubs of America and to Freedoms Foundation at Valley Forge. Over the years, Canter gave a good deal of money to the college.

One Memorial Day, when I was an Associate at Dewey Ballantine, I took my two kids Linda and Douglas to view our local parade. There we bumped into a colleague of mine, a fellow associate, at the firm. We saw each other frequently at the office and occasionally met on the train. I'll call him Smith for purposes of this narrative. I turned to my kids and said, "I'd like you to meet my friend, Mr. Smith and his two children." With that, he turned to his two kids and said, "Kids, I'd like you to meet my friend, Mr. Joseph."

How revealing. The Mr. Joseph to whom he mistakenly referred was the only Jewish partner in the firm. It was obvious that in the workings of his mind, he thought of me first as a Jew and secondly as a friend or a colleague.

Permit me to share with you my five favorite samples of Jewish humor:

> The great English sculptor, Jacob Epstein, was on the Queens Honors List and was to be knighted. All of the candidates for Knighthood were summoned to Buckingham Palace for instruction and preparation for the great event. The candidates were told they would be called up one by one in turn. Each candidate would kneel on a red velvet pillow. The Queen would tap the candidate on both shoulders with a large sword and address the candidate in Latin. Each candidate would then respond with a prescribed Latin litany which they were given and enjoined to memorize. The rite would then be concluded.

On the appointed day, the ceremony began and went without a hitch until Epstein was called up. He kneeled on the pillow; the Queen tapped him on both shoulders; she addressed him in Latin.

It was Epstein's time to respond. The great man's mind went completely blank. Seconds passed though it seemed like the lapse of an eternity. He realized he had to say something. He uttered: "*Mahnishtanah halilah hazeh meecall halaylot.*"*

The Queen turned to her Lord Chamberlain and said, "Why is this knight different from all other knights?"

The final act of a traveling circus, in the center ring, was a performance by the strongman. He started his act by taking an enormous steel bar and, holding it over his head, turned it into a perfect circle. The crowd roared its approval. Next, he took a Volkswagen automobile and, lifting it with one hand, raised it over his head and twirled it on his finger. The crowd exploded with approval. Finally, he took an orange and held it over his head and squeezed it absolutely dry. He then turned to the audience and said that he had a bank cashier's check, payable to the order of bearer, for $10,000 if anyone in the audience could get one more drop out of that orange. A big strapping brute got out of the bleachers, walked to the center of the ring and squeezed that orange as hard as he could. Not a drop. A very slightly built man, well dressed in a three piece suit, then emerged from the stands, took the orange from the strongman and squeezed it with his left hand and he didn't get but one drop, he got three drops of juice coming out of that orange. The crowd was amazed. The strongman was aghast. The strongman turned to him and said, "Tell me, sir, what do you do for a living? Are you a strongman in some circus?" The man responded by saying, "No. I am a professional fund raiser for the United Jewish Appeal."

This fellow is celebrating his thirty-fifth wedding anniversary and his wife as an anniversary present gave him a brand new hat.

---

* Hebrew for "Why is this night different from all other nights?"—asked by the youngest child present at the Passover Seder table.

That day, he took the day off and he went to the races. When he got home, his wife asked him, "Well, what happened? How did you do?"

"I looked at the card and in the first race is a horse by the name of High Hat. On a hunch, I bet twenty dollars on the nose to win. By God, the horse comes in and wins!

"The next race I looked at the card and there is a horse running by the name of Sombrero. I put all my money on Sombrero to win. And by God, he came in.

"In the third race, a horse is running by the name of Green Beret. I bet it all. The same thing happened! In the fourth race, a horse by the name of Brown Derby is running. The same thing over again! In the fifth race, a horse by the name of Tam O'Shanter. In the sixth race, a horse by the name of Panama Hattie and in the seventh race, a horse by the name of Fedora. The horse wins again!

"I now have $27,500 in winnings. In the eighth and last race, there is a horse by the name of Chateau. I placed all the $27,500 on Chateau to win. The horse came in last. I lost all my money."

His wife says to him, "You idiot! You imbecile! Chateau means house in French. You were thinking of chapeau meaning hat."

"Oh, my God!"

"So what was the name of the horse that won?" his wife asked.

"Some Japanese horse—by the name of Yamika."

A newly ordained Rabbi is given his first job as an assistant to a veteran—a truly experienced clergyman. After many weeks of apprenticeship, the senior Rabbi turns to the youngster and says, "I think you are ready to do the sermon next Friday night." At the appointed time, the youngster delivers the sermon and, in the robing room following the service, he asks his senior for a critique. The elder clergyman says, "Your organization of the material was superb. Your sermon was substantive and reflected the deep scholarly research you put into it. Your reference to scripture was instructive and the moral message couldn't have been better. However brilliant your sermon, you delivered it in a monotone. The congregation ultimately nodded off. You've got to get excitement, enthusiasm, spontaneity and drama into the sermon. Try it again next week."

Following the next week's sermon the robing room critique takes place. The senior reports, "Again, your material was superbly researched and organized. The way you wove in references to scripture and drew your moral message was brilliant. But, I regret to say again, you spoke in a dead monotone. If you are going to succeed you are going to have to be spontaneous and inject spirit, excitement and enthusiasm into your message. You must loosen up. I have a suggestion. I noticed that as you spoke you punctuated your speech with periodic sips from the water carafe. Next week I suggest you fill the carafe with gin. It is colorless. No one will be able to tell the difference, and it may relax you. Try it."

The youngster did. At the post-service critique the following week, the senior clergyman is ecstatic. "Your sermon was magnificent. The organization, the reference to scriptures, the moral lessons imparted—all brilliant. And, what's more—you had the members of the congregation at the edge of their seats. You could hear a pin drop. They were rapt in attention. Excitement permeated the synagogue. You were fantastic. Congratulations! There is one thing, though, David SLEW Goliath. He didn't KICK THE SHIT OUT OF HIM!"

Two Jewish men who were partners in a retail business were invited to a fancy Bar Mitzvah. They needed to buy formal wear. They looked at newspaper ads to find a suitable place to buy tuxedos when one of them came up with a bright idea. He said; "Our friend Pincus is in the business of manufacturing tuxes. Why don't we go up to his loft, get fitted out and we can get them wholesale." They repaired to their friend's loft and were duly measured. They were told that the formal suits came in two colors—jet black and midnight blue. They were rather emphatic in choosing the black.

The Saturday of the Bar Mitzvah came, the suits were delivered, and were put on. The two partners were walking to synagogue. They happened to bump into three nuns on the street. One of the men turned to one of the nuns and said, "Excuse me, sister, but we are slightly color blind. Can you tell us whether these suits are jet black or midnight blue?"

"They are clearly blue," the nun responded.

"Thank you very much." The two men walked on.

One of the nuns turned to the eldest of the three and said, "Mother, I never knew that Jews conversed in Latin." "Really." "Yes, as those two men walked away, I distinctly heard one say to the other, "Marcus, Pincus, Fuctus."

Henry Schaffer was one of the smartest and best-informed people I ever met. He was self-educated. He never graduated from grammar school, let alone high school. When he was a small boy, his father died. Henry had to help his mother run the family owned grocery store. He did not go to school. The truant officer was constantly on the prowl looking for him. Henry eluded his pursuer.

He wound up owning a chain of grocery stores. He sold them for a small fortune to a very large grocery chain. He retained the leaseholds or ownership in the real estate on which the stores operated. He sublet them to the purchaser. The real estate turned out to be as valuable as the operating business.

Henry and his wife Sally were unpretentious, self-effacing and wholly without airs. They were Schenectadians. They were Jewish.

On the day I was elected Chairman of the Board of Union College (the first Jewish person to hold that post), I am told, Henry said, "Union College had changed dramatically for the better." He made a gift of $5 million to the school.

I have been a member of the Friars Club for over thirty-five years. The Club has a beautiful home on East 55th Street. The food is great. The atmosphere is informal, warm and friendly. Members are connected in some way with the entertainment industry.

One evening on the way home from the office, I decided to stop at the Friars for a drink and the smoking of a good cigar in its second floor bar. I stumbled into a jazz session. Freddie Roman, one of the top officers—the Dean—of the Friars is a renowned and hilarious comedian. He introduced the Jazz quartet. He mentioned that they had just returned from performing in Ireland and made some very funny remarks about Jews in Ireland. He and I happened to walk out together. I told him a story, which, as it turned out, he had never heard before. Yogi Berra, the catcher for the New York Yankees, and Gil MacDougal, third baseman, were at the cage taking batting practice before a scheduled game. MacDougal told Yogi that they had just elected Robert Briscoe, a Jew, mayor of Dublin. Yogi looked up with a cherubic smile and said, "Only in America!"

Freddie had a real good laugh, and he said he was going to use my story in one of his routines. I felt great. Talk about taking coals to Newcastle!

CHAPTER 9

Married and Still Laughing

The late Henny Youngman, when asked about the secret to his long marriage, said, "We take time to go to a restaurant two times a week. A little candlelight, dinner, soft music and dancing. She goes Tuesdays. I go Fridays."

"Why are you so sad, Hank?"
"My wife said she wouldn't talk to me for thirty days."
"Why should that make you sad?"
"Today is her last day!"

The news media featured a convict's daring daylight escape from prison and his voluntary return and surrender later that evening. When reporters asked him why he had come back, he said, "The minute I sneaked home to see my wife, the first thing she said was, 'Where have you been? You escaped eight hours ago!'"

Rushing into his home, a man yells to his wife, "Charlotte, pack up your things, I just won the New York Lottery?"

Charlotte says, "Shall I pack for warm weather or cold weather?"

The husband replies, "I don't care. Just so long as you're out of the house by noon!"

A man steps into an elevator. The woman in the elevator looks at him and says, "You look like my fourth husband."

"Fourth husband!? How many husbands have you had, lady?" She replies coyly, "Three so far."

I was never *not* married. Or so it seems. I met Felice in 1943. I was thirteen, she, two years younger. I first saw her at a baseball game in which I was a participant, she part of the group of young girls cheering us on. I was a member of our AZA team. AZA stood for Aleph Zadek Aleph. What that stood for I don't remember. But AZA was an organization for Jewish boys. A few years later I would become president of our local chapter. Felice had long platinum blonde hair in those days. Beautiful. It was love at first sight.

A short time thereafter I called on her at her home at 185 Park Boulevard in Malverne, New York. I was in my Boy Scout uniform. I was a "tenderfoot," the lowest rank. Later I became an Eagle Scout, the highest rank. Her mother invited me into their living room and served a cup of hot cocoa. Her mother was an attractive woman just over forty years of age. As young as I was, I figured that the apple does not fall far from the tree. The dye was cast. I was in hot pursuit. I invited Felice to the proms at Union College. I did what I could to prepare myself to be lucky. Eight years later we were married in that very room. Good whiskey—not cocoa—was served then.

In June of 1990 I was feted at a fundraising affair under the auspices of the Anti-Defamation League. I was given their Human Relations Award. Felice's mother was there that night. When I accepted my award in brief remarks I acknowledged her presence and said, "Behind any successful man stands a proud wife—and an astonished mother-in-law."

If I were a Henny Youngman, I might say Felice and I have enjoyed twenty-six years of happily married life. We recently celebrated our 55th wedding anniversary. Wheeb (that's my pet name for her), only kidding.

Talking about long married life, I like the story about a golf foursome teeing off at the start of the 11th hole, which is adjacent to a public road. Just then, a funeral procession passes by. One of the golfer's drops his club, removes his golf cap and holds it over his heart in silent meditation for a full moment. One of his companions said, "Jack, that was very sensitive and most thoughtful of you." To which Jack responded, "That's the least I can do—after all, I was married to the woman for thirty-five years."

When I was a student at the Judge Advocate General's School at the University of Virginia, Felice and I lived in a very nice apartment constructed out of the basement of a private house situated on a pond in Charlottesville. I came home for lunch every day. Felice was then pregnant with Linda, our first child. Twenty-five years later, we were sitting with a group of friends. I was reminiscing about our years in Charlottesville and waxing eloquent about how wonderful it was to be able to come home and have lunch prepared by Felice. At that point Felice erupted. She was emphatic in stating that the worst part of our life in Virginia was the fact that I was home for lunch every day. It was God awful. I was in a state of shock! She had never mentioned this to me before. I was living in a fool's paradise. Goes to show. Different perceptions. Different strokes for different folks.

Sometime in the late 1960's when I was slaving away at the task of building our law firm, I came home one evening and told Felice that I needed a vacation. I was overworked. I was overwrought. I was a basket case, on the verge of a nervous breakdown. She was game. She suggested that we start planning a vacation then and there. I told her she didn't understand. I needed to leave on vacation NOW. She called her mother who lived only a couple of miles away. Eva picked up our two kids and looked after them. Felice and I boarded the next plane for Bermuda.

The first day in Bermuda I called the office every hour or so. The second day I called twice. The third day, I called once. After that I didn't call at all. I was "chilling out" although I don't think we used that terminology then.

One day, after we had been in Bermuda for over a week, we were strolling around the harbor in Hamilton. A British naval vessel was docked there and was holding an "open house." Members of the public were welcomed aboard and encouraged to look around. There was a rather handsome, full-bearded Englishman strolling about in a fashionable tweed suit with a poodle in one arm and a very attractive woman on his other arm. I walked over to him and said: "Excuse me, sir. I couldn't help overhearing you mentioning that you were on the *Ocean Monarch*, the ship bound for New York in a few days. My wife and I are thinking of possibly booking passage. We have never really cruised before. Is it rough for folks who are not seasoned sailors?" He responded in his reserved British accent, "It does get a bit choppy out there, you know." I said, "what about the food on board. Is it good?" "It's standard fare—nothing special." "What about the entertainment on the ship?" "Nothing especially exciting." The man continued to damn the ship with faint praise. This got my hackles up. Then and there I decided. We left the ship, walked across the road to the Cunard Line and booked passage for the two of us.

As we boarded the ship a few days later, I was handed an envelope. I opened it. At the time, I was pretty full of myself—impressed with my own importance.

I turned to Felice with great pride and said, "they must have checked up on me—we've been assigned to the Captain's table!"

That evening when we were seated at the Captain's table, one of the stewards came over and told us that the Captain would not be able to join us because his duties required him to remain on the bridge. We were, however, invited to join the Captain, in his quarters, the following evening—black tie—for cocktails. Not bad!

All dolled up, Felice and I showed up at the appointed hour. And we were welcomed by the Captain. Who was he? None other than the full-bearded Englishman in tweeds!

When the subject of jewelry comes up in conversation, I have two stories I enjoy telling back-to-back:

> To the great charity ball of the season, the buxom dowager, Mrs. Klopnick, wore a huge diamond pendant. And in the ladies powder room at the Hotel Pierre, all the women crowded around her to get a closer look at the glistening gem. The dowager boasted, "This happens to be the third largest diamond in the whole world. The largest is the Queen of England's. Then comes the Onassis. Then comes this one, which is called the Klopnick."
>
> "What a jewel!"
>
> "How lucky you are!"
>
> "Wait, nothing in life is that easy," said the dowager. "Unfortunately, with the fabulous Klopnick diamond I have received the famous Klopnick curse."
>
> The ladies were silent for but a second. "And, what is the Klopnick curse?"
>
> The dowager sighed, "Mr. Klopnick."

> A woman making arrangements with an artist to sit for her portrait said to him, "Although I have only a few items of jewelry, I want this painting to show me wearing diamond rings and earrings, an emerald brooch, and a multi-strand necklace of pearls that look like they are priceless."

"I can do this all right," said the artist. "But do you mind telling me why you want this, when apparently you do not particularly care for jewelry?"

"You see, if I die first," said the woman, "and my husband marries again, I want that second wife to go out of her mind trying to find out where he hid the jewels!"

When Felice and I were both students at Cornell University, she as an undergraduate and I as a law student, we lived in downtown Ithaca on North Geneva Street. Our bedroom was an unheated enclosed porch. Each morning we would choose up to see who would jump out of bed into our frigid room, run into the kitchen, turn on the oven, open the door so we could don our clothes before some heat.

One evening we decided to go to the movies. There was a film showing that we both really wanted to see. On the way to the theater we stopped and bought some candy. When we got to the movie house, the price of admission had been raised so that we simply did not have enough money. Disappointed, we went on home with our bag of candy.

I thought of this incident years later when government service brought us to Washington and to our apartment in the Watergate. One evening we were invited to the White House for a musicale by President and Mrs. Reagan. Mel Torme, the Velvet Fog, performed. June Allyson, the movie actress, was also there. Of course, there were other dignitaries as well. As they say in the Virginia Slims ads, "we'd come a long way Baby!"

Felice and I attended the festivities surrounding the twenty-fifth reunion of my graduation from the Cornell Law School. Included in the programs was a class dinner for members of the Class of '53. The dinner planning committee asked each alumnus in turn to get up and say a few words. One by one, my erstwhile classmates got up and told about their successes and accomplishments since leaving Cornell. When my turn came I got up and opened with the observation that after twenty-five years, one's classmates had grown so bald and so fat that they hardly recognized YOU. I then told them that I was completely overcome by nostalgia. I was sitting at the table with my two law school roommates—Bernard Rosen on my left and Felice Burns on my right. Felice spontaneously jumped to her feet and exclaimed, "But we were married!" She did not intend to be funny. But, everyone had a good laugh. Oh, how our mores have changed since then.

CHAPTER 10

Kids Are a (Serious) Laughing Matter

Preacher: "Do you say your prayers at night, little boy?"
Tommy: "Yes, Sir."
Preacher: "And do you always say them in the morning, too?"
Tommy: "No sir. I ain't scared in the daytime."

The teacher was giving a talk on science. "Can anyone tell me," she asked, "why lightning never strikes the same place twice?"

"That's because the same place isn't there after lightning strikes it," a little girl said.

"Johnny, can you tell me the difference between perseverance and obstinacy?"

"One is a strong will, and the other is a strong won't."

"Tommy, what is a synonym?" the teacher asked.

"A synonym," said Tommy, wisely, "is a word you use when you can't spell the other one."

"If your mother gave you two apples and told you to give one to your brother, would you give him the little one or the big one?"

"Do you mean my little brother or my big one?"

My book of humor, *Laughing Stock*, was dedicated "to the great spirit of volunteerism which permeates our national culture, a uniquely American phenomenon, and to the countless volunteers across our land who give of their resources, talent and experiences to help others less fortunate than they." As early as 1838, Alexis De Tocqueville said, "I have often seen Americans making big and true sacrifices for the public good and I have noticed hundreds of times that whenever the need arises, they never fail to lend a hand to one another . . ."

As one of our nation's volunteers, I have been engaged in a labor of love for twenty five years. I have served as a Member of the Board of Governors of Boys & Girls Clubs of America since 1982. For two years (2001 and 2002) I served as Chairman of the Board of Governors. When I first got into the movement, the organization was called Boys Clubs of America. In 1990, we became Boys & Girls Clubs of America. When I mention this to people, they often quickly surmise that we must have been sued to force us to make the change. Actually, the opposite is true. We were sued to stop us from changing our name. The complaining party was an outfit called Girls Clubs of America. I suggested that we hire Rudy Giuliani and his partner and sidekick, Denny Young, as our lawyers. They were then in private practice. They handled the case well and settled it in such a manner that we could indeed change our name as we wished. And we did so.

Today, the Boys & Girls Club movement annually serves some 4,600,000 youngsters, 64% of whom are from minority families. 55% of the kids are boys; 45% girls. The movement has over 3,900 facilities in 50 states of the Union, in Puerto Rico and the Virgin Islands and in United States military installations around the world. The movement today has an aggregate annual budget exceeding $1 billion dollars.

Club facilities include traditional stand alone locations, schools, public housing, military bases, Native American lands and houses of worship. The programs work, thanks to more than 47,000 trained adult professional staff, 140,000 program volunteers and over 30,000 board volunteers.

Boys and Girls Clubs of America traces its roots to the founding in 1860 of the first Boys Club, the Dashaway Club, in Hartford, Connecticut. One hundred years ago, in 1906, 53 local Boys Clubs banded together to form the national federation.

During my service on the Board of Governors, I traveled the country—crossed and recrossed the nation—as one of the movement's principal spokespersons. I have been privileged to work closely with Roxanne Spillett, the able, inspirational and indefatigable President, and with a blue ribbon Board of men and women which includes giants of American industry as well as such celebrities as multiple Academy Award winner, Denzel Washington, baseball icon, Hank Aaron, and baseball great, Ken Griffey, Jr. Yankee Alex (A-Rod) Rodriguez is one of the movement's principal ambassadors.

No doubt, the movement has changed America. Our alumni include great figures in the arts, in the military, in politics, in business, in the professions, in entertainment, in athletics—in all walks of life. They are leaders in their communities and on the national stage. Over half of the alumni say the Boys and Girls Clubs literally saved their lives.

I remember so well when only seven years ago, we opened our 2,000th club in Las Vegas, Nevada, established through the generosity of Andre Agassi. General Colin Powell, whom I was instrumental in recruiting to our board of governors, spoke eloquently at the opening. He pointed out that it cost a fortune to build prisons and that, for a fraction of the cost, we could and should build more and more facilities for kids. He noted that clubs keep kids from winding up in the criminal justice system and, instead, assist kids to become participating, productive, knowledgeable and caring citizens.

Following the opening of the club ceremonies, we repaired to a beautiful golf club in Las Vegas for a luncheon. I was asked to say a few words. I said that while in Las Vegas, I had gone to check out the local schools. I said that this is what I overheard in a fifth grade classroom:

> Teacher: "What is a monarchy?"
> Student: "A people governed by a King."
> Teacher: "Who would reign if the King would die?"
> Student: "The Queen."
> Teacher: "And if the Queen should die?"
> Student: Pause—"The Jack?"

This tickled the audience. I went on to a serious exposition of the work of the clubs around the nation.

The Annual Conference of Boys & Girls Clubs of America in 2001 was held in New York City. I was a recently elected Chairman of the Board of Governors and was tapped to deliver the opening keynote address. There were over 3,000 Boys & Girls Club professionals and volunteers from all over the United States in attendance. I opened by welcoming them to the "Big Apple" and by forewarning them about the trickiness of New York taxicabs. I told two stories:

> Climbing out of a cab one day, Carol Burnett, the comedienne, inadvertently caught her coat in the door. As the driver continued on his way, unaware of the accident, Carol was obliged to run alongside the moving vehicle to avoid being pulled off her feet. A quick-thinking passerby, noticing her plight, hailed the cab and alerted the driver. Having released Miss Burnett's coat, the driver asked her anxiously, "Are you all right?"
>
> "Yes," she replied, still gasping for breath, "but how much more do I owe you?"

> A taxi was creeping slowly through rush-hour traffic, and the passenger was already late.
>
> "Please," he told the driver, "Can't you go any faster?"
>
> "Sure I can," the hack replied. "But I'm not allowed to leave the cab."

On any number of occasions, during a speech for Boys & Girls Clubs, I have used the following story to hook my audience and get its attention:

> A man telephoned his friend. "Hello," a little boy answers in a whisper.
>
> "I'd like to talk with your father. Is he there?"
>
> Whisper: "Yes, but he can't come to the telephone. He's busy."
>
> "Is your mother there?" "Yes," in a whisper.
>
> "Can I speak with her?"
>
> (All in a whisper.) "No, she can't come to the phone either. She's busy too."
>
> "Is there another grown-up there?"

(In a whisper.) "Yes, the firemen."

"Can I talk to a fireman?"

(In a whisper.) "No, they're too busy to come to the phone."

"Is there any other adult there?

(In a whisper.) "Yes, the policemen are here."

"Can I talk to one of the policemen?"

(In a whisper.) "No, they're too busy to come to the phone."

(With impatience.) "For God's sake, what are they all so busy with?"

(In a whisper) "They're looking for me."

One year ago, the International Centre for Missing & Exploited Children held a meeting of the Board in Brussels, Belgium. We were hosted by my fellow board member, Daniel Cardon, Baron de Lichtbuer, at a lavish party held in a palace once occupied by Charles V. In introducing me, Daniel took the occasion to provide us with the history of the palace and regaled us with a number of stories about Charles V.

When my turn came, I mentioned that I felt very humble in the palace's atmosphere of millennia of history. After all, our country was relatively quite new. I did say, however, that while I could not talk about Charles V, I was in Washington, D.C., and was able to bring all of them greetings from George the Second. It got a good hearty laugh. Having gotten their attention and broken the ice, I went on to talk turkey about the Centre and its important programs.

My work on behalf of children includes my service as a member of the Board of Directors of the Council for Unity. I am chairman emeritus having served for many years as chairman.

For thirty years in the New York City school system, the Council for Unity, with its youth empowerment curriculum and after-school activities, has been preventing violence, stopping vandalism, providing a real alternative to gang membership and teaching inter-racial, inter-ethnic, inter-religious and inter-cultural understanding in the best diversity awareness program in the country.

Today, the Council has 6,000 participants in its program in 55 sites in the New York City school system. The kids are a diverse group speaking well over 50 different languages. Many are recent immigrants. Most are on the lowest rung of the socio-economic ladder. The program works. Ninety percent of its members go to college.

On two occasions—one the Annual Dinner of Boys & Girls Clubs of America, the other a Council for Unity fundraising dinner—in decrying prejudice, hatred and bigotry, I invoked the lyrics of the late Oscar Hammerstein from *South Pacific*. Lieutenant Cable falls in love with a Polynesian girl. He sings:

> It's not born in you. It happens after you're born.
> You've got to be taught to hate and fear.
> You've got to be taught from year to year.
> It's got to be drummed in your dear little ear.
> You've got to be carefully taught.
> You've got to be taught to be afraid.
> Of people whose eyes are oddly made and
> People whose skin is a different shade.
> You've got to be carefully taught.
> You've got to be taught before it's too late,
> Before you are six or seven or eight,
> To hate all of the people your relatives hate.
> You've got to be carefully taught.
> You've got to be carefully taught.

In each instance, I concluded that the good news is that if prejudice is not inborn but is taught, it can be untaught. And that is precisely what these organizations are doing—unteaching in very effective ways.

CHAPTER 11

Even Lawyers Laugh

The man was facing trial and possible imprisonment. "I know the evidence is against me," he told his lawyer, "but I've got $100,000 in cash to fight this case."

"You'll never go to prison with that amount of money," the lawyer assured him.

He didn't. He went there broke.

"And what is a contingency fee?" asked a client of a lawyer.

"A contingency fee to a lawyer means if I don't win your case, I get nothing. If I do win it, you get nothing. See?"

Prosecutor: *Did you kill the victim?*

Defendant: *No, I did not.*

Prosecutor: *Are you aware of the penalties for perjury?*

Defendant: *Yes I* am. *And it's a hell of a lot lower than the penalty for murder!"*

"Are you a lawyer?"

"Yes."

"How much do you charge?"

"A hundred dollars for four questions."

"Isn't that awfully expensive?"

"Yes. And what's your fourth question?"

Stanley Lesser and I started and built a great law firm. We opened the doors to our practice on September 1st, 1960. The name of the firm was Burns & Lesser. Stanley knew someone who was in the business of selling food and drink through vending machines. He needed a lawyer. And he agreed to pay us a MONTHLY RETAINER. It was $200 per month. His account and file number was 1,001. We didn't want to start with #001 lest we reveal that we were indeed neophytes.

Account and file number 1,002 was a fellow by the name of Higgins who was the night clerk at the Towers Hotel in Brooklyn Heights. I slept at the Towers, in stretches of a couple of nights a week. I'd work until the wee hours of the morning at Dewey, Ballantine. When I arrived at the Towers, I was frazzled, exhausted and bedraggled. One very early morning Higgins told me he needed a lawyer. His sister Marie had died and he required help in handling her estate. I told him his timing was perfect. In a few days, I would have my own law firm. I could surely help him. On September 1st, opening day, Higgins made an appearance. Our office at 55 Liberty Street consisted of an office for me, one for Stanley, a conference room, a small space for files and a small reception area. The furniture and books were in but the floors were plain concrete as the carpeting had not yet arrived. Higgins looked at me and asked to see Mr. Burns. He didn't recognize me! There I was, bright eyed and bushy-tailed with a freshly starched shirt and well-pressed suit. I bore no resemblance to the washed out rag that appeared at the Towers on a regular basis.

When I think back on that first day, I am reminded of the story told by a successful old lawyer:

> "I had just installed myself in my office," he said, "had purchased a phone and had primed myself for my first client who might come

along when, through the glass of my door, I saw a shadow. Yes, it was doubtless someone to see me. Picture me, then, grabbing the nice, shiny receiver of my new phone and plunging into an imaginary conversation along the following lines:

'Yes, Mr. Saxe,' I was saying as the stranger entered the office, 'I'll attend to that corporate matter for you. Mr. James had me on the phone this morning and wanted me to settle a damage suit, but I had to put him off, as I was too busy with other cases. But I'll manage to sandwich your case in between the others somehow. Yes, Yes, all right. Goodbye.'

"Being sure, then that I had duly impressed my prospective client, I hung up the receiver and turned to him."

"Excuse me, sir," the man said, "but I'm from the telephone company. I've come to connect your phone."

How did Burns & Lesser come about? How did it happen?

As you now know, I was an officer in Army JAG from the summer of 1954 to the spring of 1957. Felice's father, my father-in-law, Charlie Bernstein, was a member of a Masonic lodge in Brooklyn. George Lesser, Stanley's father, was also a member of the same lodge. George would regale my father-in-law with stories about his marvelous son, Stanley, who was a first lieutenant in the Army JAG stationed at the Pentagon in Washington. He boasted about how brilliant and accomplished his son was. Charlie would counter with a panegyric about his fabulous son-in-law who was also a first lieutenant in Army JAG and also was stationed at the Pentagon. This badinage between them went on for some time. Finally, they resolved that the two young men should meet and become friends. They had so much in common. They were the same age. Both were married to fine young women. Both were lawyers, etc., etc., etc.

George told Stanley to look me up. Charlie made a point of suggesting that I seek Stanley out and befriend him. Being red-blooded, normal, headstrong young men in our mid-twenties, we AVOIDED EACH OTHER LIKE THE PLAGUE.

Oh, we knew each other to be sure. We occasionally met on the badminton court, at softball games and on the touch football field. But we did not socialize.

In March of 1957, I was separated from the Army and began my employment at the prestigious law firm of Dewey, Ballantine, Bushby, Palmer & Wood. George Bove, the office manager (who one day years later would become the office manager of our law firm), assigned and showed me to a small room, maybe as large as 9 feet by 12 feet, which I was to share with another young lawyer. I opened the door and there, at one of the two desks jammed into the room, sat no one other than Stan Lesser.

This meeting changed our lives. We lawyered in that room. We toiled. We slaved. We also dreamed. And we dreamed great dreams. One day we would have our own law firm with its own high standards of excellence and ethics, with real camaraderie and collegiality, with great morale and an atmosphere that was not stuffy.

We were each earning $17,000 per year at Dewey, Ballantine. We each had two children. Neither of our wives was working at that time (they would later both be teachers). They were rearing the children full time. We quit our jobs, gave up our salaries, borrowed $5,000 from George Lesser and $5,000 from Herman Burns and struck out on our own. Over the years, people complimented us for our courage, our pluck, our entrepreneurism and our perseverance. Nonsense. Looking back on it now, it was simply an act of INSANITY.

But we were lucky. True, every day we prepared ourselves to be lucky, but lucky we were. Did our dreams come true? I think so. When I left it to join the Department of Justice twenty-five years and a few months later, the firm had a solid practice, a fine reputation and had grown to over one hundred lawyers.

I left Burns, Summit, Rovins and Feldesmen at the end of the calendar year 1985. Stan Lesser had withdrawn from the firm ten years earlier, effective December 31st, 1975, to accept appointment as a United States Bankruptcy Judge. Stan had suffered two heart attacks and it was thought that retiring from the active and stressful practice of law would prolong his life. Sadly, Stan died in 1987.

My last year at the firm witnessed the firm's revenues and net profits at the highest levels to that point in time. In my last report, as head of the firm, delivered in early 1985, I had this to say:

> Looking back on 1984, there is no doubt that it was a busy, productive, gratifying and, in many respects, an enjoyable year. In my view, the firm had its strongest year: in handling a variety of complex and challenging matters with its standard of excellence to the satisfaction of happy clients; in acquiring new and important clients; in the extracurricular activities of our partners and associates, ranging from the selection of judges, the raising of substantial funds for charities, leadership in philanthropic organizations, school board activities on national, state and local levels, Bar Association work, teaching, writing, lecturing and *pro bono* lawyering; in our increasingly active athletic programs which embrace basketball, softball and running; and in our many social events, including our magnificent annual dinner, holiday party, and parties large and small at the drop of a hat on any pretext.

> To be frank, we have been struggling for several years in trying to develop a simple brochure to describe our firm. It may be impossible to capsulize the unusual qualities of our firm—its emphasis on imagination, innovation and creativity, its concentration on human relationships *inter se* and with clients, its belief in the nobility and the majesty of the law (despite its occasional warts) and its determination to make important societal contributions, both within and without the firm. It's hard to explain what we mean when we say our firm has big-firm muscle but maintains small-firm mentality.

In December 1984, I wrote about the firm's annual dinner:

> Our firm's Annual Dinner took place on Sunday evening, November 11, 1984, at the elegant Garden City Hotel. It was a smashing success—like others!*
>
> The personal warmth, the camaraderie, the friendship and the mutual respect which permeated the party were moving.
>
> By any standard of measurement, ours is a successful enterprise: firm revenues; firm profits; our magnificent physical plant; our winning performance; client satisfaction; our reputation in our community and beyond; our record for community and public service; the quality and diversity of our clientele; and the caliber of our partners and associates.
>
> I have long believed that we would not have achieved as we have without the solid underpinning of the family and team atmosphere which we are fortunate to enjoy. Let's continue to strive to maintain what we have. Let's keep working on improving our interpersonal relationships. In the final analysis, that's what really counts. It sounds corny; but believe me, it is so true.

How did we help make our dream come true? How did we prepare ourselves to be lucky?

One thing I can say for sure, humor contributed mightily to the outcome. We had a firm motto: "When in doubt, mumble." We had a firm logo depicting the Quetzal bird and proclaiming the desire to maintain status quo. We had a

---

* Held at the Four Seasons, Orsinis, The Atrium, Windows on the World, La Cirque, The St. Regis, The Helmsley Palace, The Century Café and The Water Club.

house organ, not surprisingly named "Mumbles," which was published once a month without fail. "Mumbles" was started in January 1973. We had athletic uniforms adorned with the "Mumbles" patch. When I left the firm, "Mumbles" was still going strong. The firm also published a "Morning Mumbles," a one-sheet newsletter, every single business day, to keep people informed on a very current basis about important goings-on.

I was a frequent contributor to "Mumbles" as were so many members and associates. I wrote about such varied matters as professional responsibility; the responsibilities of the firm's associates to the firm; the responsibility of the firm to associates; fundamentals of law practice, ethical standards of lawyers, the necessity of keeping clients' confidences and secrets; humorous stories, anecdotes and articles; book reviews; the redemption of thousands of Ethiopian Jews; a quiz on our United States Presidents; the birth of a new nation Namibia; and, annually, a report on the state of the firm. "Mumbles" also contained countless firm songs, the brilliant lyrics of which were written by my late partner Mortimer Felsinger, as well as many original cartoons. And, of course, it reported on our legal practice, cases won and lost (mostly won), office development and growth and personnel and personal news.

People were encouraged to contribute. We made fun of ourselves and sometimes lampooned each other. For example, my head was shown on the corpulent body of King Farouk of Egypt and on the emaciated body of Mahatma Gandhi. Becoming editor of "Mumbles" was a matter of distinction and a sign that you were going places within the firm. While everyone participated, as I think back on it, the spark plugs behind "Mumbles'" success were Alan Hyman, Tanya Tesa, Erwin Cherovsky and my very good friend and late partner, Everett Frohlich, each of whom served as editor.

Alan Hyman is today a senior partner at Proskauer Rose LLP (the firm to which I was recruited by Alan and others following my government service, which proves the old adage, "what goes around comes around"). Alan today is one of the most respected bankruptcy lawyers in the country. He cut his teeth assisting me in the 1970's with handling the Black Watch Farm matter, to that point in time the largest bankruptcy case in the history of New York State. I am very proud of him.

Tanya Tesa recently retired as an executive vice president of the Economic Development Corporation of the City of New York in charge of managing the lion's share of the properties owned by the City of New York and responsible for generating annual revenues of over $60 million for the city. I am extraordinarily proud of her achievements.

In bidding me farewell in 1984, Tanya had this to say in a "Mumbles" piece:

> On December 31, 1985, Arnold Burns will be leaving the firm he started just over 25 years ago. I first met him in October of 1972 when George

> Bove, then Office Manager, introduced me to him as a candidate for a job. We quickly reached an agreement and thus began an employment relationship which over the years became a collaboration rooted in deep friendship.
>
> The firm has come a long way since then. Revenues, physical plant, legal and non-legal personnel, clientele, *pro bono publico* activities and philanthropic work burgeoned and then mushroomed.
>
> * * *
>
> His tangible contributions to the firm are, of course, many and will be enduring. But most of all, he worked hard at developing an atmosphere of camaraderie, mutual respect, and good feeling. "Mumbles," annual dinners, athletic teams, office parties, birthday and anniversary celebrations are some of the traditions he believed were vital to the morale and well-being of the firm.
>
> * * *

Erwin Cherovsky was a prolific contributor to "Mumbles" on an endless variety of subjects. He is today a literary agent to whom I am greatly indebted for helping me put this book into publishable form. When I left the firm, he wrote, in part, in "Mumbles:"

> Although I do not envision that Arnold will have too many casual moments at Justice, if from time to time there is a pause in the day—or evening—activities, his associates at least will have access to a raconteur of the first rank. Arnold's inventory of stories is seemingly endless, and although some are just funny, a good number have a message and bite . . .

My dear friend, the late Morris ("Morrie") Liebman, a senior partner of the prestigious law firm, Sidley & Austin, wrote of "Mumbles:" "It is refreshing to find a law firm newsletter which goes beyond the usual matters of office practice and legal development . . . We improve as lawyers as we become enriched as human beings."

Did our dreams come true? You be the judge. Everett Frohlich, wrote this editorial in "Mumbles" in 1974:

> Why does this firm have an Annual Dinner? Why do we have an event for which we dress formally; an evening in which we dine very well,

dance, intermingle and exchange small talk with each other—all in gracious surroundings?

Why does the firm sponsor intramural athletics—pitting the "jocks" (m.) and "jacques" (f) of one floor against another?

Why do we have periodic wine and cheese parties where for a short interval of time we relax together and banter and laugh with each other?

Why do we have a mid-winter holiday party; an affair at which there are no professional distinctions—a party at which we are all just friends with a common bond?

Why do we publish "Mumbles"—a journal in which we all have an opportunity to write of our professional achievements or to reminisce or to relate our experiences or try our hand at humor?

Is it our purpose to provide interludes of entertainment, fun and games? It certainly is—but as a means to a greater end! We believe that socializing together—whether in formal attire or in jeans or slacks or over a glass of wine or in journalistic endeavors—has an important effect on each of us. In these activities we reveal ourselves to each other with all our strengths and foibles; we become less brittle, more understandable and even likeable! We are people with distinct personalities and backgrounds. We are individuals banded together for a common purpose: a collegial effort to serve our clients. Toward that end we ask for your enthusiastic and active participation. But above all, we hope that you continue to enjoy each of our social interludes.

Yes. Humor was part of the mucilage which kept us together working in harmony toward common goals. We took our professional responsibilities very seriously. We never took ourselves too seriously. We laughed with and at each other. We had fun.

For well over ten years I served as George Steinbrenner's lawyer as well as the principal lawyer for the New York Yankees. When I was a boy, my father, who was an avid baseball fan, would take me to Yankee Stadium. We sat in the center field bleachers and saw the great Joe DiMaggio loping like a gazelle around center field. On several occasions before his death, I met and chatted with Joe

DiMaggio in George's office. Sitting in George's office at the Stadium watching the game was always a thrill for me—a long way from the bleachers.

My first legal assignment for George was a tough one. He had been banned from baseball for LIFE by Commissioner Fay Vincent. The conduct for which George was punished grew out of a bitter dispute in which he was engaged with Dave Winfield, a star outfielder for the Yankees. George and Fay were both graduates of Williams College. They were students at Williams at the same time. Notwithstanding, there was no love lost between them. They mixed like oil and water. Got along like a wild cat and a feral dog. Both dug in for the fight of the century. Without going into boring details, suffice it to say that, with the assistance of my partner Randy Levine, I was successful in persuading Commissioner Vincent to reinstate George. Vincent was represented by former Deputy Attorney General and former United States District Court Judge Harold ("Ace") Tyler, an outstanding lawyer and a fine human being.

Some years ago I invited George Steinbrenner to deliver the keynote address at the annual conference of Boys & Girls Clubs of America, convened that year in San Diego. I introduced George in glowing terms. I told the large audience that George was one of the most charitable men I had ever known, many of his good works performed anonymously. I went on to talk about many of George's other fine qualities—all true. I then asked each member of the audience to stand, raise his or her right hand and to take an oath. I asked each of them to pledge that they would never repeat any of the nice things I said about George. I explained that he had a reputation to uphold—a reputation for being an old meanie, a pretty tough ogre. That got a good laugh.

George opened by explaining how he happened to be chosen to deliver the opener. He explained that Arnie Burns asked him if he believed in free speech, and when he responded enthusiastically in the affirmative, Arnie asked him to come to San Diego and deliver a free speech. As I remember it, George delivered one hell of a talk. It and he were so well received.

When I served as Deputy Attorney General, John ("Jack") Lawn was Administrator of the Drug Enforcement Administration, part of the Department of Justice. One day, Jack (who became a good friend and remains a close friend to this day) came by with Dave Winfield with whom DEA was collaborating on drug prevention. Dave stands 6 feet 6 inches tall. He had his mother with him. She stood about 4½ feet tall. We had a real good chat. When we were through, I called in the Justice Department photographer and asked if it would be all right to do a photo. Dave said, "fine," and stood up to have his picture snapped with me. I told him then I had no desire to be photographed with him . . . I wanted a picture with his mother! That was it. Dave and I became friends and we remain real good friends to this day. I still have the photo. His mom, since passed on, was a great lady.

Now to close the loop. Years later, after the Steinbrenner-Winfield contretemps, and, after George's restoration to participation in baseball, I arranged for a secret meeting between them at the St. Moritz Hotel on Central Park South. I engineered a rapprochement between them. I did good. And, I am proud that they are both friends of mine and now friendly to each other.

When I left the practice of law in January of 1999, I received the following letter from George:

> *Dear Arnie,*
>
> *I was a bit startled by your letter of January 11 but I can certainly understand and you are totally accurate when you say that you are making the move when you are at the top of the game. You are one of a unique number of men that I have idolized for some time and you have been a great friend, a great confidant, a great advisor and a great representative in the legal profession for both myself and the Yankees. I certainly hope that this move accomplishes for you what you want out of it and I send my very best wishes and hopes for that being the case.*
>
> *Best personal regards,*
> George

In my book—and this is my book—George is the greatest sports impresario in history. So there, we have the making of a mutual admiration society.

In 1959 I was still an associate lawyer at the Dewey Ballantine firm. I was dammed lucky. The firm was a large firm (by the standards at the time), and I wound up working directly with Thomas E. Dewey, the former New York Governor who headed the firm.

We were working on a case on behalf of our client, New York Hospital, which had a facility in White Plains. The State, exercising the power of eminent domain, had taken a swath of the Hospital's property and had built on it an entry ramp for the New York Thruway. We were hired to challenge the taking as illegal. The legal issues were fascinating, but not particularly important to recount here.

The hospital, represented by other counsel, sued the State and lost the case. We took an appeal to the Appellate Division and won. The State appealed to the New York Court of Appeals. Paxton Blair, the Solicitor General of New York, submitted his Court of Appeals brief. I was tasked with the job of writing our answering brief. Our brief had to be served no later than on a particular Wednesday.

Because Governor Dewey was a perfectionist, one strove to avoid any possible mistakes. I could have mailed our brief to the Attorney General's office, and service would have been effected. But to ensure that the brief was properly and timely served, I instructed a member of the firm's managing clerk's office to fly to Albany on Wednesday and personally deliver the brief to the Attorney General. Wednesday happened to be Yom Kippur, the holiest day of the year for Jewish people. I was out of the office and in my synagogue. When I came in on Thursday morning, I called in the clerk to make sure all had gone smoothly. He came to my office and when I asked him how he effected service, he responded by saying "Mr. Burns, I goofed." "What do you mean you goofed? What happened?" I responded. He then told me that he went to the Secretary of State's office and served the papers there. He never got near the Attorney General's office. When I asked him what the Secretary of State had to say, he told me that the Secretary of State said he was in the wrong place and that he should go to the A.G.'s office. He said he thought they were trying to trick him, so he insisted on leaving the papers and left. GOVERNOR THOMAS E. DEWEY WAS IN DEFAULT.

My dumb mistake was not to have mailed a copy of the brief *in addition* to having had it delivered. But now, what to do?

I picked up the phone and I called the Attorney General of New York, then Louis Lefkowitz. I explained what happened. I then told him as I see it, there are three alternatives: One, for me to go in, come clean and tell Governor Dewey what happened; two, for me to throw myself out the window of my 28th floor office and kill myself; and three, for the Attorney General to go find my brief in the Secretary of State's office and sign a receipt showing he had received it on time.

I said "General, alternative one is utterly out of the question. That leaves alternatives two and three. It's your call. My life is in your hands."

Attorney General Lefkowitz could not have been nicer. He told me he didn't want my death on his hands. He promised then and there to track down our answering brief, to acknowledge receipt in timely fashion and to never divulge to Governor Dewy what had happened. And he delivered. What a mensch! What a generous way to treat a 29 year old fledgling lawyer!

When the time came to argue the New York Hospital case in the Court of Appeals, Governor Dewey and I were going to take the 9AM Empire State Limited from Grand Central to Albany. I set my alarm the night before our departure with plenty of time to spare—ample time to train from our home in West Hempstead, Long Island, to Penn Station and, from there, to Grand Central. As luck would have it, my alarm clock mechanism did not function properly and the alarm never sounded. I woke eventually. When I saw the time, I panicked. No chance of getting the train. I picked up the phone and called my father-in-law, Charlie Bernstein, who lived not more than two miles from us. I said "Dad, wake up, do not put on any clothes, throw a coat over your pajamas and come get me in your car. We are going to Grand Central. Don't ask questions. Just get going."

Can you imagine my state of mind? It was clear to me that if I missed the Albany train, my legal career was OVER. Well, we made it. I was there 15 minutes before the train time. GOVERNOR DEWEY WAS NOT. As minutes ticked off the train departure time, I panicked again. Where I had been in deadly fear that I would never get to Albany at all, I now was in deadly fear that the Governor would not show and that I would have to argue the case.

At 8:59 AM, I spotted the impeccably groomed Governor in his Hamburg hat sauntering down the platform as loose as a goose. We made the train, we argued the case, and we won it.

On the train to Albany we bumped into George Shapiro, a distinguished lawyer who had served as Counsel to the Governor during the Dewey administration. The Governor introduced me to George. I was very impressionable and quite impressed. Little did I realize then that George and I would become law partners when I joined the Proskauer firm in 1988.

Governor Dewey and I took the plane home. We were feeling pretty good. The argument had gone well. As the person who had done all the research and prepared the brief, I knew the case cold, like the back of my hand. It would have been natural for me to have felt that I could have presented our case as well as, if not better than, the Governor who had studied our brief, who read the principal case precedents and who had been fully briefed by me. NOT SO. The Governor's presentation was superb in all respects. I could not have held a candle to him.

On the plane back, the Governor reminisced about the time Charles Evans Hughes returned to the practice of law after service as Governor of New York. Dewey accompanied him to Albany as his assistant when Hughes argued his first case in the Court of Appeals post governorship. (Hughes later became an Associate Justice and then Chief Justice of the Supreme Court of the United States.) According to Dewey, Hughes predicted that Dewey would be Governor of New York one day. The New York Hospital case was Dewey's first case following his tenure as Governor. (Dewey aspired to become the leading lawyer in the nation, much like John W. Davis—who ran unsuccessfully for President against Calvin Coolidge in 1924—had been. He would have made it for sure had it not been for his untimely death.) He turned to me on the plane and said that "one day Arnold you will be governor of our State." What a compliment! He was a fine human being. He was a great lawyer. He was a fabulous role model. He was an inspiring mentor. He was a lousy prognosticator.

When I left Dewey, Ballantine, Governor Dewey gave me a lot of pointers about starting a firm. He also gave me some good advice. I'll never forget what he said: "Arnold, a lawyer who practices law for money is not worth a damn. And a lawyer who practices law and who does not make a lot of money as a consequence thereof is also not worth a damn."

As a lawyer defending persons accused of criminal behavior or of conduct transgressing governmental regulations, I have often told the following story to clients to make the point that delay, continuances and passage of time work in the defendant's favor:

> A Russian peasant was caught poaching on the Tsar's hunting preserve. The secret police beat him to a bloody pulp. In handcuffs and leg irons, he was dragged before the Tsar. When told of the offense, the Tsar ordered the man executed on the spot. The peasant importuned: "Your Majesty, if you spare my life, I will teach your pet bear to dance."
>
> The Tsar granted a reprieve, but was emphatic in making it clear that if the bear did not dance in 90 days, the man would be summarily executed. The man breathed a sigh of relief and, when released, went straight home. He told his wife about his close call with death. She remonstrated with him, told him he was an idiot to make such a promise to the Tsar, and said he was certainly doomed.
>
> The peasant demurred. "Look, there are four possibilities," he said. "First, during the 90 day period I may die of natural causes. Second, during the 90-day period, the Tsar may die of natural causes. Third, during the 90-day period the bear may die of natural causes. And, finally, during the 90-day period, that f* * *ing bear will dance!"

When a successful outcome occurred, I would say to them, "You see, the bear did dance!"

One of my favorite lawyers' stories:

> A man keeps his appointment with a lawyer. He tells the lawyer about the dispute he is having with a business partner which has been unresolvable. He tells the attorney the whole story. The lawyer advises that he has a very strong case which the lawyer will win for him in court. The man gets up, tells the lawyer he is not going to hire him and starts to walk out. The lawyer asks, "Why are you leaving? I've told you, you have an open and shut case. Are you not intending to institute suit?"
>
> "Well, no—the reason is—you see—I told you my business partner's version of the case—his side of the story."

I loved the law. The law has been very very good to me. Very generous to me. I like to think I have been good to the law.

Managing a large law firm is not easy. By and large, lawyers are independent thinkers and rugged individualists; are egocentric and often egomaniacal; and are generally pains in the neck. When I was managing partner of our firm, I at first thought of myself as an orchestra leader harmonizing cacophonous sounds coming from different quarters. In time, I realized that was not quite right. No, I was a lion tamer whose job it was to stand in the center of a cage with a whip and keep the lions from eating each other, and, importantly, from eating me. Time passed. That was not quite it. I realized that I was really more like a hockey goalie, ducking the hard round black puck being constantly directed at my head from different angles by diverse persons. No, still not quite right. One day, I picked up the *New York Times* and read that the managing partner of one of our very prestigious and substantial law firms in New York City had stepped down. Yes. He captured the essence of what it was like to be managing partner. He was quoted as saying it was just like being a lone hydrant on a New York City street overrun by hundreds of dogs!

Joking aside, I subscribe to the view expressed by Harrison Tweed, once President of the Association of the Bar of the City of New York, who said (and this is a paraphrase): Lawyers are better to work with, fight with, play with and drink with than any other species of mankind.

In 1998 while I was still an active lawyer at the Proskauer firm, my partner, Gregg Mashberg, asked me to address its young lawyers. The branch offices in Washington, D.C., Boca Raton, Florida and Los Angeles, California, were hooked up via video conference. This is how I started my talk:

"Sit back relax. You don't have to take notes. And I promise you one thing; I am certainly not going to say anything profound. That's for sure.

"I know for sure that you won't remember anything I'm going to say today. Do you know how I know that? For years I worked very closely with one of our colleagues here, Eric Levine. Eric and I worked together day-in day-out, week-in week-out, month-in month-out. And I was asked to give a commencement speech in South Carolina. I was working on crafting this speech. I was trying to get a certain tempo and cadence for the speech. And I remembered I had given a commencement speech at Hofstra Law School years before in 1987 . . . 86 or 87. I asked my secretary if she could dig up a copy of that speech for me so I could see how I handled this before and she couldn't find it in our files. Being very resourceful, she called the Hofstra Law School and they sent me a recording of my speech.

"So, I'm sitting in my office working on my speech, listening to this recording. I wanted to get the cadence of how I delivered this particular message, and Eric Levin walked in. He says, "What are you doing?" I say listening to this speech. He sat for a minute or two and then said my God! I was there. I graduated from Hofstra Law School that year. I've forgotten you and everything you had said!

"To add insult to injury, I was Chairman of the Board at Union College and I personally handed him his college diploma and he forgot that too!

"He tried to assuage my feelings, 'cause after all, I am a senior partner, by telling me the following day that he had discussed it with his wife Melissa and she remembered."

I went on to deliver a motivational and inspirational talk the distilled message of which was "prepare yourself to be lucky." Years after I left the Proskauer firm, I was invited to speak to their then current crop of young lawyers and I was pleased to reprise my earlier talk, updated and modified, to be sure.

It all started at Myron Taylor Hall the home of the Cornell Law School on the Cornell University Campus in Ithaca, New York. For as long as I can remember, I wanted to be a lawyer. My father was one of three brothers. He was the handsome, charismatic, athletic type. He was even on the stage for a brief period. He never went to college, but his two brothers became successful lawyers. One graduated from Harvard Law School in 1912. Franklin D. Roosevelt, 32nd President of the United States, was a classmate. His brothers' success and lifestyle influenced me. They seemed to have much more interesting, exciting and cushier lives than my father did. My Dad was a retail jeweler for most of his working life.

My mother and father wanted me to go to the Harvard Law School. I had other plans. My sweetheart, Felice, was a Cornell undergraduate. I decided I was going to the Cornell Law School so that Felice and I could be together. I had some explaining to do when my mother found a blank Harvard law application in my sock drawer. I stuck to my guns. I matriculated at Cornell.

What luck! Cornell University is huge—one of the major centers of learning in the United States. But the Cornell Law School is a small college. We had 180 students in each of the three classes, or a total of just over 500 students in the entire school. The Law School is not much larger today. The entering class at Harvard each year has many more students than the whole Cornell Law School.

The small college atmosphere was thoroughly conducive to studying law. There was genuine interaction between students and faculty. I truly enjoyed law school. I revered my professors—men like Rudolf Schlesinger, John W. MacDonald, W. David Curtiss and Ernest Warren. They taught. They inspired. They motivated. At that time, there was no course in professional ethics. But in my view, one couldn't sit through classes with these men without getting a sense of ethics through osmosis. It permeated the classroom air.

At the beginning of my law studies, I was intimidated by the whole process. My prayer was that I would not flunk out and disgrace myself and my parents. I was a kid from a small college. There were some mighty impressive people in my class. Very loquacious. Very articulate. They overwhelmed me. I did not think I could compete.

The first day of law school I got the assignment for one of my courses off the bulletin board. I went home and did it. It took me all night. I told Felice that law school was really tough and that I would probably never see her again, because I'd been up all night for just one course. When I got to class, I learned that I had done the assignment *FOR THE ENTIRE MONTH!*

At the end of the first year, I finished tenth in my class. I was genuinely astonished. With my confidence established, I finished fourth in my class behind Mark Fields, Ted Munroe and Stan Springer. I could have finished first if I hadn't been so scared that first year.

I qualified to compete for the *Cornell Law Review* (then called the *Cornell Law Quarterly*) and was named Note Editor. The law school also published its magazine *The Cornell Law Forum*.

When I was serving as Deputy Attorney General, I was invited to speak at a law school function in Ithaca. I opened my talk by explaining that I was actually visiting at the law school the day I was notified that the President wanted to appoint me to the Justice Department. I was walking down one of the halls of the school heading toward the offices of the Cornell Law Forum when one of the students caught up with me and said there was a phone call for me from Washington, D.C. I described the experience by saying, "A funny thing happened to me on my way to the Forum."

When I was at Cornell, I had a pretty fair photographic memory. Today I can hardly remember what I had for breakfast. When I took the final examination in Procedure, a course taught by Ernie Warren, I answered each question by referring to cases by name and in some instances by citations. When I got to the last question, I wrote something like, "this issue was decided by Judge Cardozo, as Chief Judge of the New York Court of Appeals, in a case involving tortious interference, the name of which escapes me for the moment." Professor Warren called me in. He was flabbergasted. He said had he not been in the room watching me take the exam, he would have thought I wrote the answers in the library with the legal volumes at my elbow. Twenty-five years later at a reunion weekend, he spoke of this incident with relish.

My time at law school was very successful. I got a first-class legal education. Whatever I have achieved as a lawyer, I owe to the Cornell Law School. And, I got my girl. Felice and I were married at the conclusion of my first year of law school study.

At the law firm I founded with Stan Lesser humor contributed mightily to its rapid success. Shown here is our logo, depicting the Quetzal bird; our motto—"When In Doubt, Mumble;" and our coat at arms, Status Quo.

Mumbles photo depicting my head on the body of Mahatma Gandhi.

Mumbles photo depicting my head on the body of King Farouk of Egypt.

My grandson Scott, Union College Class of '14, with Randy Levine, President of the New York Yankees.

My grandson Brendan with George Steinbrenner at Yankee Stadium.

My daughter Linda and me at Union College on the occasion of her 25th and my 50th college reunion.

CHAPTER 12

In the Wilds of Africa

A man on a Safari in deepest Africa became separated from his group and was hopelessly lost in the vast desert. He walked and walked in the hot sun. Finally, totally exhausted and dehydrated, he fell to the ground. Just then he saw what he thought was a mirage. There in the middle of the desert was a Jewish delicatessen, "Cohen and Levine."

With all the strength he could muster he crawled and crept toward the mirage. And, sure enough, it was no mirage at all. Indeed, there was a deli there. He went in and ordered a hot pastrami sandwich on rye, Dr. Brown's celery tonic, a side of slaw, sour pickles and tomatoes, cheesecake and coffee. He surfeited himself. He got up to pay his tab and, to his astonishment, there was a wild boar at the cash register, taking checks, collecting money and making change.

The man turned to the proprietor, Mr. Cohen, and said, "This is miraculous, we can take this wild boar to New York and make a fortune. We can put him in the circus, get him spots on televised variety shows, take him to Hollywood. Cohen said, "Nothing doing." The man persisted. "You don't understand. We can become rich with this act. "No," said Cohen, "you don't understand. This is not a wild boar at all. IT'S MY PARTNER LEVINE. HE CALLED THE WITCH DOCTOR A SCHMUCK!"

In 1970 I was hired by a successful entrepreneur who lived in our home town, West Hempstead, Long Island. His name was Aaron Knopf. He had made a fortune with a chain of retail camera stores. He had taken his money and invested it in an amethyst mine in Southwest Africa. He wanted to take his company, owner and operator of the mine, public and hired me and my firm to represent him. As part of our due diligence, I traveled with him to Windhoek, Southwest Africa's principal city, and to its environs to make sure there was a mine, amethyst and a *bona fide* operating company.

While there, thanks in large measure to Aaron Knopf, I met, befriended and was befriended by all the wrong people. The wrong people included, Bishop Colin Winter, Anglican Bishop of Southwest Africa, Clemens Kapuuo, Chief of the Herero Tribe, Johannes Keroia, the Chief's Secretary, and a man by the name of James Endicott.

Five years later, in 1975, the South African apartheid government which controlled Southwest Africa and its vast Kalahari Desert decided to give up its control and to establish a new independent country there to be named Namibia. The territory was the size of France and Germany combined. It had a population of only 750,000. The wrong people had become the right people. Chief Kapuuo, the odds-on favorite to become first president of the new nation, was invited to participate at a constitutional convention to be convened in Windhoek, the purpose of which was to craft and adopt a constitution for the new nation. Kapuuo agreed to come on two conditions. Condition one was that he be permitted to bring his headmen to the proceedings. The Hereros were split into sub-tribes each led by a headman. One of the sub-tribes lived in the Kakoveld, a vast region where they lived just as they did in the Stone Age. The South African government said OK. Condition two was that Kapuuo be allowed to hire and bring to the convention one, Arnold Burns, from New York City to act as his counselor, advocate and lawyer. The South African government said ABSOLUTELY NOT. Kapuuo stuck to his guns. The South Africans would not relent. They were at an impasse. Finally, as Kapuuo was truly a key player, the South Africans caved in. I was duly credentialed and did, indeed, undertake the representation of the Herero tribe at the Constitutional Convention.

I spent a good bit of time in Namibia. I spent a lot of time there with Aaron Knopf. He told me a story I have told many, many times since:

> A man who had been trying to break into the acting game for years and years finally got a call from his agent. He said there was a small part available at the Long Wharf Theater in New Haven, Connecticut, and it was a speaking part. It was small, but a beginning. He would have to go out on stage on cue and say, "Hark, hear that cannon roar!"

> The would-be actor took the train to New Haven and went to the men's room and practiced the entire way up. "**Hark**, hear that cannon roar." No. "Hark **hear** that cannon roar!" No, that was not quite right. "Hark, hear that **cannon** roar." No not it. "Hark, hear that cannon **roar**!."
>
> Yes. He practiced and finally had it down pat. He reported to the Long Wharf Theater, met the manager and the manager told him when he tapped him on the shoulder, he was to walk out in the center of the stage and recite his line. At the appropriate moment the manager gave him the high sign. He walked out in the center of the stage and an enormous cannon went off. He turned to the audience and said, "What the hell was that?!"

At the end of the 19th century, when Germany decided to colonize what became German Southwest Africa, they sent troops. Seven of the eight tribes which inhabited the land rolled over and played dead. Not so with the Hereros. The Herero men are tall, handsome, strong, dignified and courageous. When required they were warriors. They fought the Germans. They were overpowered by a superior force and by greater arms and equipment. They were interned in camps. And an official government order issued in Berlin—the Von Treute order—which I have seen and read in the original German. It decreed the execution of every tenth Herero male. This is probably the first case of genocide in recorded history.

At the convention it was suggested that each of the 8 tribes and the 9th tribe, namely the white Caucasians, should have representation in proportion to their population. My brief for the Hereros was that, in calculating their number for this purpose, they should be credited with the population the Hereros would have had if they had not been decimated by the Germans. We didn't win that very poignant point.

In 1976 Chief Kapuuo and Johannes Keroia spent Thanksgiving with me and family in New York. For Christmas that year, I gave the Chief a bulletproof vest. There was a lot of political strife going on and I felt his life was in danger. I was prescient. Unhappily, while he was at home in his own backyard, without his vest on, he was assassinated by a person or persons who have never been identified. A year or so later, James Endicott was murdered by a person or persons unknown.

With Kapuuo's death, I gave up my lawyering for the tribe. But we did succeed in birthing a new nation—Namibia. Apartheid was ended in the new country. And the end of apartheid there was the beginning of the end of apartheid in the Republic of South Africa itself. It was the precursor of the new South Africa with Nelson Mandela freed and leading the government there.

On one trip to Namibia I was accompanied by my law partner Stuart Schwartz. He and I shared a room at the only decent hotel in Windhoek. One evening there was a knock on our door. I opened it to see two very young comely and shapely black women there. They tried to force their way into our room. Stuart and I pushed against the door as hard as we could. We succeeded in getting the door closed. We barricaded the door with furniture. We were scared. It was obvious the authorities were trying to set us up for criminal charges based on inter-racial fornication. They wanted us compromised and out of there. Draconian laws were then still in effect. If we hadn't gotten that door closed, we might still be in prison in South Africa!

The bright, bubbling new missionary studied the grave faces of the African natives sitting before him. "We are brothers together in Christ, children of the same Lord, blessed with immortal souls now and forever and into the resurrection . . . Amen."

From the ranks of the natives came in unison, "*Bombaloobo . . .*"

"And, my children, you must dedicate yourselves never, never to spill the blood of your neighbors!"

"Bombaloobo," crooned the congregation.

"And you must love each other, and even your enemies . . ."

"Bombaloobo! Bombaloobo!"

"May the good Lord bless and keep you," said Father Hallinan.

"Bombaloobo . . ."

As the missionary gathered up his Bible and his alb, Mogambo, the chief of the tribe, came before him bowing.

"Chief Mogambo," exclaimed Father Hallinan, "I don't think I have ever had a more sincere reception . . . I will come back next Sunday."

"Yes, yes," said Chief Mogambo. "Go in peace. And as you go down the trail to get into your Jeep, please be careful . . ."

"Of what, Mogambo?"

"Not to step into the elephant *bombalooba*."

AFTERWORD

As you can see, I have expended most of my energy during my lifetime in preparation for, and in, the practice of law. As a lawyer I have litigated cases and argued appeals (including two in the Supreme Court of the United States) across the country; I have practiced corporate and securities law; criminal law (both on the prosecution and defense sides); government regulatory and enforcement law, sports law and bankruptcy law. I had a piece of the Oklahoma bombing case. I was in the "Filegate" case representing members of the United States Secret Service. No question. The practice of law, both in the private and public sectors, defines my life. The practice of law was very good to me. And, as I have said, I like to think I've been good to it. Over the years, I have trained and mentored many lawyers younger than I. Protégés of mine have become leaders at the Bar in government, academe, industry and private practice. I helped build two great law firms in my time at the Bar.

But the truth of the matter is that I have received the most gratification in my life by activities outside law practice and outside business. A few years ago, our nuclear family, Felice, Linda, Doug, Brendan, Leah, Scott and I visited Monticello, Thomas Jefferson's home in Charlottesville, Virginia. We were struck by the fact that Jefferson's tombstone states that he was the author of the Virginia Bill of Religious Freedoms, a founder of the University of Virginia and author of the Declaration of Independence. No mention is made of the fact that he was President of the United States. I would like to be remembered not for my achievements in law or in business but for serving others as the following:

- Captain, United States Army, JAGC
- Deputy Attorney General of the United States
- Chairman of the Board of Boys & Girls Clubs of America
- Chairman of the Board of the International Centre for Missing & Exploited Children
- Chairman of the Board of Union College
- Chairman of the Board of Freedoms Foundation at Valley Forge
- Son, brother, husband, father and grandfather.

INDEX

T

U

V

W

Y